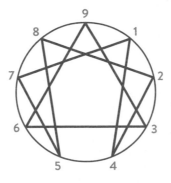

THE
ENNEAGRAM
&
YOU

Understand Your Personality Type and
How It Can Transform Your Relationships

Gina Gomez

ADAMS MEDIA
New York London Toronto Sydney New Delhi

*To you, the reader, and to the countless people like
you and me, on the endless quest for understanding
ourselves and our relationships.*

Adams Media
An Imprint of Simon & Schuster, Inc.
57 Littlefield Street
Avon, Massachusetts 02322

First Adams Media hardcover edition March 2020

ADAMS MEDIA and colophon are trademarks of Simon & Schuster.

For information about special discounts for bulk purchases, please contact Simon &
Schuster Special Sales at 1-866-506-1949 or business@simonandschuster.com.

The Simon & Schuster Speakers Bureau can bring authors to your live event.
For more information or to book an event contact the Simon & Schuster Speakers
Bureau at 1-866-248-3049 or visit our website at www.simonspeakers.com.

Interior design by Priscilla Yuen
Interior images © 123RF/lamika, undrey; Simon & Schuster, Inc.

Manufactured in the United States of America

10 9 8 7 6 5 4 3 2 1

Library of Congress Cataloging-in-Publication Data has been applied for.

ISBN 978-1-5072-1272-1
ISBN 978-1-5072-1273-8 (ebook)

CONTENTS

INTRODUCTION

All over the world, people are trying to figure out why they act the way they do. Everyone has asked themselves at some point in their life at least one of these questions: "Why do I always go along with what other people want instead of speaking up for myself?" "Why does she shut down when I express emotion?" "Why does he get nervous when I want to change plans?" "How does she always seem to know the perfect thing to say?" "Why does my boss get so angry if I make one tiny mistake?"

Now you have a way to see the motivation behind your behavior and others': the Enneagram. This fascinating system is a way to describe and understand yourself and others using nine different personality Types. You determine your Type by taking the Enneagram Quiz. So, for example, you will be able to see why you're so level-headed in a crisis or why your partner always seems to anticipate your every need in the most thoughtful way. Likewise, when you understand where certain frustrating behaviors come from, you can begin to see that most of them are coping mechanisms that developed during childhood. There's no one to blame and there's no reason for you to shame yourself or others for the challenging parts of your personality. The information you learn from the Enneagram will help you practice more compassion for yourself and those around you.

The Enneagram can teach you things about yourself that you never knew until you learned your Type. You'll have "aha" moments again and again as you recognize patterns in your life. You won't want to stop discovering all the nuances of your personality. As you learn more, other people will come to mind—your spouse, your parents, or maybe even your boss or someone you work with. You immediately want to know what their Enneagram Type is. You can see the potential that exists to have even better relationships with these people if you know their Type.

Think about the many times you've ruminated over a conversation that went poorly or had an encounter with someone that left you scratching your head in confusion. Those experiences can be exhausting, frustrating, and overwhelming—but it doesn't have to be that way. You hold in your hands a guide to navigating through any and all of your relationships, using self-awareness and compassion for others as a foundation. Find out what you have in common with others when it comes to strengths and challenges, what disputes are likely to come up so you can anticipate and avoid them, and how to handle conflict effectively by approaching difficult situations mindfully.

This book will be a source of knowledge for you forever. You'll be able to reference it when you start a new job, go out on dates, make a new friend, or work out issues with your partner. The Enneagram can guide you on your path to self-improvement and growth—no matter what your Type.

QUIZ:
WHAT IS YOUR ENNEAGRAM TYPE?

Let's determine what Enneagram Type you are.

Before you begin the following quiz, take a few deep breaths and clear your mind. Allow yourself to be as honest as you can be in your self-assessment—don't answer based on how you'd like to see yourself or what you think the "right" answers are. There's no need to judge yourself—simply answer honestly to get the most accurate results.

To figure out your Type, follow these steps:

1 Read through each of the following quizzes and check the box (Agree, Neutral, or Disagree) that best applies to you or your situation.

2 When you finish each group, tally the number of checkmarks in each column.

3 Then multiply the number of Agree checkmarks by 2, Neutral checkmarks by 1, and Disagree checkmarks by 0 and add up your total for that quiz and move onto the next one.

4 When you finish Quizzes A–I, move onto the Scoring the Quizzes section for further instruction.

QUIZ A	AGREE	NEUTRAL	DISAGREE
I am sensitive.			
I strive to have a unique style.			
I look for meaning in just about everything.			
I am often misunderstood.			
I am highly creative.			
Being authentic is important even if it means I'm not popular.			
I tend to feel jealous of others, even though I can't explain why.			
I am comfortable with dark and intense emotions.			
I can be pretty sentimental and long for the past.			
I value self-awareness, following my heart, and always staying true to who I am.			
TALLY	x 2	x 1	x 0
FINAL TALLY			

TOTAL SCORE =
(Agree + Neutral + Disagree)

QUIZ B	AGREE	NEUTRAL	DISAGREE
When I have an idea, I just go for it!			
I love thinking about my next adventure.			
I'm pretty good at finding the silver lining in most situations.			
My independence is very important to me.			
New experiences make me come alive!			
I can be pretty spontaneous and fun-loving.			
I am most likely to keep my options open.			
I loathe being bored.			
I value pleasure, variety, and my freedom.			
I am highly resilient and can bounce back from upsetting setbacks.			
TALLY	x 2	x 1	x 0
FINAL TALLY			

TOTAL SCORE =
(Agree + Neutral + Disagree)

QUIZ C	AGREE	NEUTRAL	DISAGREE
I can be pretty hard on myself.			
Several people in my life come to me for advice.			
I'm excellent at finding mistakes (typos, things out of place, etc.).			
It's difficult for me to relax when I know there is so much to get done.			
I find myself feeling frustrated and irritated when things are not done correctly.			
I believe that there is a right way to do everything.			
I'm great at finding what needs to be fixed or corrected.			
I am independent and can get things done on my own rather than depend on others.			
I'm a self-disciplined person.			
I value truth, justice, and living by my values.			
TALLY			
	x 2	x 1	x 0
FINAL TALLY			

TOTAL SCORE =
(Agree + Neutral + Disagree)

QUIZ D	AGREE	NEUTRAL	DISAGREE
I am known for my strength.			
I have a tough exterior but most don't realize that I am quite soft on the inside.			
I want the outside world to understand that I am a force to be reckoned with.			
Confrontation does not bother me.			
I feel as though I can't let my guard down.			
People have sometimes referred to me as being "too much" or coming on too strongly.			
I often feel as though I need to protect myself, my loved ones, and those less fortunate.			
I feel an overwhelming responsibility to always be a pillar of strength.			
When I'm stressed, I tend to overanalyze to regain some form of control.			
I value strength, leadership, and candor.			
TALLY	x 2	x 1	x 0
FINAL TALLY			

TOTAL SCORE =
(Agree + Neutral + Disagree)

QUIZ E	AGREE	NEUTRAL	DISAGREE
Having success is very important to me.			
Other people's opinions matter to me.			
I work hard at trying to earn the respect and admiration of others.			
It doesn't have to be perfect; it just needs to get done!			
I like to set goals for myself.			
Encouragement and affirmations from my peers feel amazing!			
I know how to work a room.			
I have a very competitive spirit; I like to win!			
I enjoy encouraging others and helping them live up to their potential.			
I value reaching my goals, achieving something, and being admired.			
TALLY	x 2	x 1	x 0
FINAL TALLY			

TOTAL SCORE =
(Agree + Neutral + Disagree)

QUIZ F	AGREE	NEUTRAL	DISAGREE
I think that knowledge is everything.			
I want to connect with others but I simultaneously fear the energy it requires.			
I need a lot of alone time to recharge, think, and learn.			
I'm more comfortable having an intellectual conversation versus an emotional one.			
I need to fully understand something before I can act on it.			
I can be a pretty private person.			
My deep well of knowledge has sometimes come across as arrogant or condescending.			
Being self-reliant is very important to me.			
I enjoy learning and pursuing my interests.			
I value innovation, privacy, and intelligence.			
TALLY	x 2	x 1	x 0
FINAL TALLY			

TOTAL SCORE =
(Agree + Neutral + Disagree) _____

QUIZ G	AGREE	NEUTRAL	DISAGREE
I prefer to let things go rather than have a confrontation.			
I am a great listener.			
I strive to live in a peaceful and calm environment.			
I enjoy being creative.			
I am accepting and inclusive.			
I wish I had more ambition.			
I am an optimist.			
I typically see the good in people.			
I can usually see all sides of a situation.			
I value serenity, optimism, and maintaining inner peace.			
TALLY	x 2	x 1	x 0
FINAL TALLY			

TOTAL SCORE =
(Agree + Neutral + Disagree) _____

QUIZ H	AGREE	NEUTRAL	DISAGREE
I am very loyal to my family and friends.			
I can be suspicious of people's motives.			
I take my responsibilities seriously.			
I am dedicated and hardworking.			
The future worries me and I can't stop obsessing over it.			
It's vital that I feel supported.			
It's difficult for me to spring into action before assessing all the possibilities.			
It takes me a fair amount of time to trust people.			
I often have daydreams or actual plans to rebel against social norms, rules, and authority figures.			
I value loyalty, being supportive, and being collaborative.			
TALLY			
	x 2	x 1	x 0
FINAL TALLY			

TOTAL SCORE = _____
(Agree + Neutral + Disagree)

QUIZ I	AGREE	NEUTRAL	DISAGREE
Being needed makes me feel proud and valuable.			
Relationships are the most important thing in my life.			
I am excellent at understanding what people need.			
In most relationships, I give more than I take.			
I tend to focus on other people's emotions.			
I tend to neglect my own needs.			
People usually come to me when they're hurting because I'm a good friend.			
It's important for me to feel needed.			
I have used flattery in the past to get people to like me.			
I value emotional closeness and human connection above all else.			
TALLY			
	x2	x1	x0
FINAL TALLY			

TOTAL SCORE =
(Agree + Neutral + Disagree)

SCORING THE QUIZZES

Now put your total score from each quiz into this chart and star the highest score.

YOUR TOTAL SCORE	
Quiz A	
Quiz B	
Quiz C	
Quiz D	
Quiz E	

YOUR TOTAL SCORE	
Quiz F	
Quiz G	
Quiz H	
Quiz I	

If you scored highest in Quiz A, you are most likely Type Four.
If you scored highest in Quiz B, you are most likely Type Seven.
If you scored highest in Quiz C, you are most likely Type One.
If you scored highest in Quiz D, you are most likely Type Eight.
If you scored highest in Quiz E, you are most likely Type Three.
If you scored highest in Quiz F, you are most likely Type Five.
If you scored highest in Quiz G, you are most likely Type Nine.
If you scored highest in Quiz H, you are most likely Type Six.
If you scored highest in Quiz I, you are most likely Type Two.

Don't worry if you have the same score for more than one quiz—that's perfectly normal. In Chapter 3, there is a comprehensive outline of each Type that will help you discern which one best describes you. Once you dig deeper into each Type, you will likely discover that you have a more dominant Type. Keep in mind that discovering your Enneagram Type is a personal journey; as eager as you might be to figure it out right away, take the time you need to ensure you Type yourself correctly.

If you're still unsure of your Type and need more guidance, consider taking a free online quiz like the one at www.eclecticenergies .com/enneagram/dotest. You could also find an Enneagram coach, like myself, to administer an Enneagram test to you. Enneagram coaches can help you determine your Type, understand Enneagram teachings, foster self-development, and strengthen your relationships.

1

Understanding the Enneagram

What Is the Enneagram?

The Enneagram is an ancient personality system made up of nine different personality Types (*ennéa* is ancient Greek for "nine"). It's similar to other personality systems out there, like the Myers-Briggs Type Indicator or StrengthsFinder, in that it has specific Types with a list of traits and behaviors. However, the Enneagram is the only personality tool that tells you *why* you have the traits and characteristics that make up your personality. It acts as a guide to show you what is motivating your behaviors, how you approach conflict, and what happens to you when you're stressed. It gives you a deeper insight into how and why your personality developed. It supports your journey to self-awareness and can help you strengthen your relationships.

ORIGINS

Though no one is sure exactly how the Enneagram began, there are a few theories. All of them involve some spiritual connection. Several Christian leaders have integrated the Enneagram into their gospel teachings.

Wherever it came from, the modernization of the Enneagram is all thanks to Oscar Ichazo, a Bolivian-born mystic. He formed a school, the Arica, where he taught the concepts to a group of about forty students. One of the students, Claudio Naranjo, brought what we know as the modern Enneagram to America in the 1960s. Since then, Enneagram teachings have spread and are now studied and practiced all over the world. With the help of modern technology and the increasing number of teachers writing books about the Enneagram, more people are now able to learn all about it.

The Enneagram Symbol

The Enneagram symbol is a geometric shape composed of three parts: a circle, a triangle in the middle of this circle, and an irregular hexagon in the center.

Located equidistantly on the circumference of the circle are nine points that represent nine different personality Types. Two lines radiate out from each of these nine Types; one line points to that Type's Security Point and the other to that Type's Stress Point.

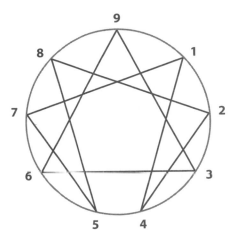

Each of the points you see is connected to a number and the numbers represent the nine different personality Types.

Enneagram Essentials

Let's cover the basics of the Enneagram to familiarize you with the different components of the system and what they can tell you about yourself and others.

THE NINE ENNEAGRAM TYPES

There are nine different personality Types in the Enneagram system. Each Type has a set of common characteristics and behaviors, along with various other components that help explain how this Type approaches the world.

Each of the nine Enneagram personality Types has been given names by various Enneagram teachers, psychologists, and authors over the years. While you're on your journey to discovering what your core Type is, don't pay much attention to any assigned names you might see. You don't want to be influenced in any way while you're trying to discover your Type.

You have one dominant or core Type that has manifested in you based on a combination of:

- The environment in which you grew up.
- The unique set of traits you were born with.

It's important to note that you do not change from one Type to another. Many aspects of your life can change, but your core Type remains the same throughout your life.

Although you have one dominant personality Type, you actually carry, to some degree, all nine Types within you. You will always return to your natural core Type, even when external or internal factors bring out your nondominant Types.

THE LINES OF SECURITY AND STRESS

Each personality Type has two lines pointing in two different directions on the Enneagram map: that Type's Security Point and its Stress Point. In Chapter 3, you'll learn more about each Type's specific Stress and Security Points. For now, here is some general information about why those points are important.

Security Points

This is the direction your personality moves in (subconsciously) when you achieve a sense of security or when you're coming out of stress and going into a sense of reprieve. This is the path toward self-awareness and self-actualization. It's here that you're able to rest your defenses and become more available to ideas, people, and experiences.

Let's use Type Eight as an example of moving toward your Security Point. When Type Eight moves in the direction of Type Two (its Security Point), they begin to let down their guard and become more open and vulnerable. They no longer are hypervigilant for who or what might hurt them.

If Type Eight develops an unhealthy connection to Type Two, they can become resentful, coercive, and manipulative to get their needs met. Type Eights can become resentful when they put themselves out there and then feel betrayed when someone uses their vulnerability against them. These are not common traits for Type Eight to have; eventually they will return to their dominant personality Type.

Stress Points

This is the direction your personality tends to go to in times of stress; you can also take on the traits and behaviors of this Type when you need to access skills and abilities for a particular situation you are in. This can feel stressful when you're not used to it. It's out of your comfort zone and you'll think about acquiring a helpful habit but find it's difficult and takes practice.

For example, let's say someone is crossing the line with a Type Two and the Type Two feels like they need to push back. When they are leaning into their Stress Point (Type Eight), they can take on a more aggressive nature usually exhibited by a Type Eight. A Type Eight is able to become assertive, stands up for what they need, and creates healthy boundaries for themselves. These traits will probably be uncomfortable for a Type Two to display until they have strengthened this connection.

Every Type can access the healthy and more challenging aspects of their Security and Stress Points. Once you identify and understand yours, you will notice that you move toward these points at various times. You may wake up feeling great and ready to take on the world, but then something unfortunate happens and now all you want to do is climb back into bed, eat a box of cookies, and yell at whoever tries to bother you.

The connections to other Types allow you to have a greater awareness and understanding of your behaviors, and to grow as a person. Whether you'd like to move away from or closer to certain behaviors, your Security and Stress Points can point you toward new skills that you have natural connections to.

WINGS

Your core Type makes up the majority of your personality, but there are other components of the Enneagram that complement your personality.

Wings are one of those components. Your Wings are the two Types adjacent to your core Type. For example, if you're a Type Five, your Wings would be Type Four and Type Six.

The characteristics of both your Wings have the potential to show up in your personality. Most people have one dominant Wing; perhaps later in life, traits from the other Wing will show up in your behavior and point of view. We're all different, so your Wings might show up at the same time.

The important thing to know about Wings is that some of their traits may be present in your life. After all, in order to fully understand yourself, it's necessary to be aware of everything that could be influencing your approach to others and to the world.

Triads and Centers

The placement of the numbers on the Enneagram circle by modern scholars helps make sense of Enneagram theory. If you connect the points to make three triangles, you can see three Triads that are grouped as follows:

- Two, Three, and Four
- Five, Six, and Seven
- Eight, Nine, and One

Each of the Triads has a dominant emotion, as defined by its Center of Intelligence. (You might see Triads named differently as you do more research on the Enneagram system.)

THREE CENTERS OF INTELLIGENCE

According to the Enneagram, there are three Centers of Intelligence within you. These Centers influence how you perceive the world and how you absorb information:

- The Body Center, also known as the Instinctual Center
- The Heart Center, also known as the Feeling Center
- The Head Center, also known as the Thinking Center

It helps to learn about the Centers in order to get a better understanding of your core motivations.

The Body Center

Types Eight, Nine, and One reside in this Center.

The Body Center relates to movement, action, gut instinct, and physical sensations in the body. It's concerned with motion, vitality, and the act of doing. The Body Center receives instinctual energy from the gut, which creates what feels like convictions that must be acted on.

The common thread between Types Eight, Nine, and One is their desire for respect, comfort, and most importantly, control.

Emotional Theme: Anger

The Types in this Center frequently try to keep some semblance of control. They are motivated by the desire to remain autonomous, which creates the need for control. When they do not achieve the independence they need, they become angry, resistant, and even demonstrate feelings of rage.

The Heart Center

Types Two, Three, and Four reside in this Center.

The Heart Center is where emotions are sensed and expressed. It enables you to connect with your feelings and the feelings of those around you. This is where emotional intelligence can be obtained and where fears of unworthiness or not being loved manifest.

The common thread between Types Two, Three, and Four is a desire for meaning, value, and most importantly, identity.

Emotional Theme: Shame

All the Types can feel shame, but the Heart Types chronically experience shame. This stems from wanting and needing approval, admiration, love, and appreciation. When these Types do not receive validation from others, they grow sad and become ashamed.

The Head Center

Types Five, Six, and Seven reside in this Center.

The Head Center relates to rationality, analysis, ideas, planning, and prioritizing. The main focus is a deep connection with mental strength, intelligence, and the ability to effortlessly understand so that they can feel prepared, knowledgeable, and safe.

The common thread between Types Five, Six, and Seven is their desire for security.

Emotional Theme: Fear

The Types in this Center are trying to calm their anxieties. This is a direct result of each of these Types not feeling safe. They need more certainty, reassurance, and opportunity to help minimize their fears. If they cannot manage to find inner peace and self-assurance, they will be overcome with irrational fears.

OTHER TRIADS

There are three other sets of important Triads to know about.

Hornevian Triad

The first one is the Hornevian Triad, which was developed by Karen Horney, a neo-Freudian psychoanalyst. She theorized that during a child's early experience, they develop three coping strategies or stances: Assertive, Compliant, and Withdrawn. It basically describes how each Type attempts to work through their inner conflict and how they meet their needs. We all have the ability to access any of these styles, but the strategy assigned to your Type is usually the one that's most dominant in your personality.

The Assertive Stance (Types Three, Seven, and Eight): Future-Focused; Represses the Past

Threes, Sevens, and Eights are all independent and self-assertive Types. They are self-starters, extroverted, and full of energy. They oppose others as a way to gain control, which can come across as assertive or aggressive. Those with an Assertive Stance are commonly outward-focused, toward a result or goal. They usually see an opportunity before most and will go after it without much contemplation or assessing how they feel about it. They are typically self-confident and feel a sense of importance in the world. When they are tense or feel challenged, they will try to get around the roadblocks. They are some of the first to take decisive action, but they tend to delay or never finish what they start.

The Compliant Stance (Types One, Two, and Six): Present-Focused; Represses the Future

Ones, Twos, and Sixes are highly aware of morals and social rules. They know what is expected of them and try their best to work through obstacles by sticking to whatever rules might be in place. They're usually responsible and ethical people who put a great deal of pressure on themselves in order to get their needs met. They can be very self-sacrificing, hardworking, and committed individuals. They tend to lose touch with themselves, making it difficult for them to trust themselves. Instead, they overcompensate by relying on external guidelines.

The Withdrawn Stance (Types Four, Five, and Nine): Past-Focused; Represses the Present

Fours, Fives, and Nines are all introspective individuals who spend a fair amount of time by themselves. They prefer it that way, as it allows them to explore their ideas and imagination without outside disturbances. They respond to obstacles by retreating and avoiding, which is also how they go about getting their needs met. They can easily become overwhelmed with the outside world and need plenty of time to withdraw in order to replenish their energies. These three Types are disconnected from the Body Center (also known as the Instinctual Center), making it difficult for them to fully be present in the moment. They are usually quiet individuals who prefer to engage with smaller groups to explore their imaginative ideas and musings.

Harmonic Triad

This Triad describes how each Type moves through adversity, trials, and conflict when their needs are not met. It includes three options: the Competency, Positive Outlook, and Reactive Approaches. We all have and use these various approaches, but usually it's the one associated with your Type that is most prevalent in your personality.

The Competency Approach (Types One, Three, and Five)

Ones, Threes, and Fives set their emotions aside when handling difficult situations. They would rather handle conflict with objectivity, rationality, and efficiency. They are usually calm and emotionally detached during a conflict but can become extremely agitated if others are not taking that same approach. Competency is critical in being able to achieve a solution during conflict, but repressing one's feelings by denying or pushing emotion out of a conflict causes its own problems. This group can easily miss out on the emotional experience of a situation that is vital to embodying compassion and empathy toward others and themselves.

The Positive Outlook Approach (Types Two, Seven, and Nine)

Twos, Sevens, and Nines are optimistic individuals who would prefer to see the world with a positive outlook. They tend to ignore negative emotions and would rather reframe unpleasant situations. They'll sweep red flags or negative feelings under the rug, deny them, or distract themselves as a way to continue to avoid conflict. This group usually struggles with trying to get their needs met and simultaneously trying to meet the needs of others. They wrestle with working through difficult obstacles. By denying or avoiding real conflict, they can inadvertently create much more serious obstacles for themselves.

On the flip side, having a positive outlook during conflict can be very beneficial to neutralizing heavy emotions.

The Reactive Approach (Types Four, Six, and Eight)

Fours, Sixes, and Eights are the most emotionally honest Types in the Enneagram. When in conflict, they are highly reactive and can become emotionally volatile under stress. They have a difficult time steadying their emotions and typically want to be met with the same intensity. Although some people think that emotions should be left out of conflict because they might distract from the "real issues," it's actually healthy to work through feelings even during conflict. If emotions get buried, they eventually reveal themselves in some other unhealthy manner. It's all a matter of releasing emotions in a way that doesn't negatively affect oneself or others.

Object Relations Triad

Object Relations is a psychoanalytic theory that says that babies form relationships with and certain expectations of their parent or caregiver, who is known as the "object," as part of the formation of the self. The Object Relations Triad describes how the way in which you experienced your relationship with your caregiver determines how you relate to the significant people in your life as an adult. For example, a Type Four who longed for a different dynamic with one or both of their caregivers will still be looking for that potential ideal relationship as an adult. Again, people have and can utilize any of these to varying degrees, but your core Type is predominantly the strongest.

Attachment (Types Three, Six, and Nine)

Threes, Sixes, and Nines are trying to stay in alignment with the world around them. They are focused on attaching themselves to a certain state of being that allows them to be content with the way things are. They do this by merging with what others want, being in agreement with a particular way of life, or trying to control and maintain their inner peace. For example, a Type Three focuses on being who others want them to be. Their sense of self is based on an attachment to their self-image in whatever form it needs to take, depending on who they are with.

Frustration (Types One, Four, and Seven)

Ones, Fours, and Sevens are idealists. They have a certain idea of how experiences, situations, and people should be or act, but are typically let down and frustrated that reality never lives up to their expectations. They build up these ideas in their head and are often left feeling disillusioned. Their frustration grows, yet they keep trying.

Rejection (Types Two, Five, and Eight)

Twos, Fives, and Eights sense that they have been or will be rejected by society or by people they care about. They tend to feel as though no one truly cares about their needs, yet they will often reject those who try to help them. To avoid being rejected, they instead offer up something they can bring to others. For example, a Type Two fears being unloved and not needed, therefore they will go to great lengths to show up for people by helping or becoming indispensable to them to avoid not being liked, accepted, and needed.

2

How the Enneagram Can Improve Your Life

Let the Enneagram Guide You

The Enneagram is a dynamic tool that allows us to understand the motivations behind what we do and say. Why is this useful? Start off by thinking back to a time when you were upset by someone's behavior or something they said. Their actions might have left you feeling rejected, angry, or unsettled in some way. Maybe you reacted with anger too, only to find out later (after they explained that they had had a terrible day at work) that what they said wasn't about you at all, but about how stressed they felt.

You immediately feel better when you've reached that kind of understanding, right? Well, what if we could avoid all that time, frustration, and misunderstanding? That's what the Enneagram provides. If you were aware of what was motivating their behavior in the first place, your understanding of the situation would be much deeper. You would have knowledge of underlying truths that could be at play with you or the other person. You would anticipate and avoid issues, slow down your reactiveness so you don't say or do things you might regret, and communicate in healthy and constructive ways. When you replace judgment with compassion, you also stop taking things so personally. The Enneagram acts as a guide that can help you navigate through your challenges—or help you avoid them in the first place, by doing the following:

- Promoting self-awareness
- Nurturing self-love
- Encouraging mindfulness
- Boosting your sense of compassion
- Improving your relationships

Let's delve into more on how these benefits of the Enneagram can change your life.

PROMOTING SELF-AWARENESS

Self-awareness and mindfulness are vital components of reflecting on yourself and your behavior. In order to accept and acknowledge that you might tend to react to certain situations in a specific way, you first have to notice that it's happening. The Enneagram lists traits and common behaviors for each Type that can promote self-awareness. For example, Ones tend to suppress their feelings, which can restrict their emotional connection to themselves and others. By bringing awareness to this, it allows them to gently observe their behavior.

Think of your personality as a chest of drawers. If you start digging around a little, you'll likely find things that you love about yourself, that give you a sense of pride or satisfaction. But if you dig a little deeper with the help of the Enneagram, you might also see parts of yourself in one particular drawer that you don't like as much, such as a tendency to be manipulative, selfish, obsessive, or passive-aggressive.

Depending on where you are on your journey of self-discovery, you might just want to shut that drawer and walk away. However, in order to develop a healthy relationship with yourself and others, you have to accept *everything* in your drawers. We all have things in our drawers that we aren't comfortable with, but they do not define you. Open all your drawers and let the light shine in. It's the only way you can practice self-awareness.

How can you become aware of some of these behaviors that might make you uncomfortable? Ask yourself questions about why you do what you do. The answers help you dig a little deeper into your motivations to understand what's beneath the surface of your behavior. Let's say you sometimes have trouble standing up for yourself. You can ask yourself, "Do I often find myself avoiding confrontation? Do I feel afraid to let others know where I stand when it comes to my own personal beliefs?" You might check in with yourself during a heated argument and ask, "Am I feeling scared? Am I feeling threatened?"

The answers to questions like these can illuminate deeply held beliefs that you keep inside. Once you know they are there, you can decide whether or not they truly align with who you are as a person. Self-awareness is truly the first step on your journey to self-discovery.

NURTURING SELF-LOVE

The most important relationship in your life is the one you have with yourself. Just as you know that it's important to take care of your physical well-being with a healthy diet and proper exercise, it is also important to take care of your mental and emotional well-being. A key way to start doing that is to practice self-love. After all, it's your responsibility to take care of yourself, be kind to yourself, and love who you are from the inside out. The Enneagram will help you foster self-love because learning more about *why* you do the things you do can give you helpful perspective and information about yourself that you can process without judgment. Be kind to yourself, celebrate how far you've come already, accept that there is pain in life, and replace judgment and criticism with compassion and self-love.

You may already show yourself love, especially if you grew up in an environment where self-love was shown and taught to you by caregivers. Even if that wasn't the case for you, it's not too late to develop your own good habits. Focusing on the future is a much more productive option than assigning blame for dysfunctional and unhealthy behavioral patterns on someone or something in the past. To start, simply extend acceptance of where you are right at this moment. Try to be grateful for everything you've been given and acknowledge that you are doing the best that you can.

Throughout your life, you will experience natural ebbs and flows in your self-love. You might wake up in the morning feeling amazing and get ready for your day by loving your body, nourishing it well, and feeling great; by the end of the day, however, you're exhausted, feeling lonely, and starting to move away from love and into behaviors that are not very loving. And that's okay. There's nothing wrong with that. The good news is that you can always bring yourself back to practicing self-love. When your self-love practice is strong, even on your darkest days, when you feel unlovable, incompetent, or inherently flawed, you're still able to acknowledge your experience and take care of your feelings as you're living them—which is, essentially, self-love.

ENCOURAGING MINDFULNESS

Mindfulness means trying to live in the present moment, not in the past (where old hurts might reside) or in the future (worrying about tomorrow rarely helps). Being mindful also includes stopping and thinking before you act. Mindfulness is a practice that you can easily implement in your daily life. Once you're aware of a behavior that you want to work on, bringing your attention to it is a way of being mindful to it. By practicing mindfulness, you're able to change your behavioral patterns.

For example, let's say you're a Type One who wants to work on softening your inner critic. You could ask yourself reflective questions, freewrite using journal prompts, or simply observe the behavior without judgment. Instead of coming down hard on yourself for something you think you could have done better, offer yourself grace and compassion. You acknowledge that for most of your life, you've felt that you had to be perfect, but now you know perfection doesn't exist. Then you can tell yourself what a great job you did, and how all the hard work and effort you put into self-improvement really speaks to how much integrity you have.

Another example is if you tend to lose your temper, such as when another car cuts you off on the road. Maybe your go-to response is to yell, curse, and work yourself up until your heart is racing and your fists are clenched. When you feel those physical reactions, take a deep breath and engage in a contemplative moment of gratitude. Thankfully, you are safe and no one was hurt by someone else's negligence and disregard.

Practicing mindfulness allows you to have compassion for yourself and others, which is another important benefit of the Enneagram.

BOOSTING YOUR SENSE OF COMPASSION

Once you become more aware and mindful of your behavior, strengths, weaknesses, and thought patterns, it will be key to practice compassion for yourself and others.

After all, we can't beat ourselves up for being human. We all have flaws, and none of us got to choose where we were born, what family we grew up in, or how we were raised.

Every person you encounter has a backstory just like you. They had challenges growing up, and they've experienced heartache and pain. Sometimes it's hard for us to imagine that about certain people, such as someone rich, someone who seems to have it all, or someone whose personality clashes with yours. You might act less than compassionately toward these people because when you're not aware of what challenges others might have gone through, you feel disconnected and less compassionate toward them.

For example, let's say you're a Type Two and you become aware that when you're feeling lonely and in need of attention, you tend to feel needy and codependent. Instead of getting down on yourself, by understanding the Enneagram and the underlying motivations behind those thoughts, you're able to see more clearly that your behavior is a result of past wounds or hurts that have not yet healed. You're able to choose to give yourself the love you didn't receive when you needed it. You're also more inclined to tend to those unmet needs on your own rather than expecting others to do it for you. You're able to release the anger you feel toward others and replace it with compassion. You begin to understand that we're all only capable of so much, and that as adults, the only person responsible for your emotions and needs is you.

Being able to treat others with compassion begins with drinking from your own well of love for yourself. Recognize any pain you have gone through and treat yourself with compassion. Talk to yourself as you would counsel a good friend. This practice helps create more patience, understanding, and healing for yourself and others.

IMPROVING YOUR RELATIONSHIPS

If you think about the most important relationships in your life, they probably fall within these three categories: family and friends, partners, and coworkers. These are the people we spend the majority of our time with. The Enneagram will help you improve your connections with all three groups in the following ways.

Harmony in the Home

Healthy family relationships encourage all members to have strategic coping mechanisms along with a healthy dose of self-worth, connection, gratitude, and acceptance. Children learn to treat others by the way they are treated at home, and home should be a place where everyone feels safe, loved, and understood.

The Enneagram acts as a guide to navigate the various personalities who are all trying to coexist in harmony under one roof. The Enneagram outlines your core fears and your core desires so you can start to understand your motivations and how they affect not only you, but those you live with as well. You will be able to access a whole new set of tools immediately, thanks to the Enneagram.

You'll learn how to approach conflict with a Type Six or what to avoid when you're in a relationship with a Type Five. You will learn how to support those you love and what to be mindful of when things get stressful. You'll be able to see your parents and siblings from an entirely different perspective, one that fosters compassion and understanding instead of judgment and criticism.

You can also extend these same practices to your friendships. You share a sense of belonging, solidarity, and connection with your friends, and they deserve your best self. After all, friends mean a great deal to you and you want to protect and strengthen your friendship bonds just as much (if not more, sometimes!) than family. Once you know your Type, you will be more aware of your strengths and challenges, and will find the best way to approach key situations with important people in your life.

Intimate Relationships

If you think about your most complicated relationships, a romantic partner probably comes to mind. It could be someone you're dating now, a former partner, or someone you've been married to for several years. These relationships can seem impossible to manage at times, even when you have a lot in common. Questions and concerns such as these race through your head:

- How will we ever make it through another argument?
- I don't understand why he keeps pulling away.
- Why does she always get angry when I'm trying to explain something to her?
- Most of the time we're great, but when we're apart, I feel anxious and scared.
- I can't remember the last time she showed me any appreciation for all that I do.

Most of these issues arise because one or both parties hasn't effectively communicated their concerns to the other. You might assume something instead of asking questions, or you might feel too scared to speak up for yourself.

You enter a relationship with a set of fundamental beliefs that you learned from your upbringing, and the other person brings a whole set of their own. Some of these principles might be the same, but it's usually the ones that are different that matter. There is a sense of comfort and safety with what we know, but anything different can create confusion and will definitely rock the boat between two people who are just trying to love each other.

The Enneagram can teach you what each Type needs within a relationship. We all have our own set of needs, and it is incredibly useful to be aware of both your own and your partner's needs. The Enneagram can also help you find out how best to love your partner, and to remember to be grateful for what both parties bring to the relationship.

Work and Career

Your coworkers are another important group of people in your life. You don't necessarily choose these people to be a part of your life, but most of us have to work, and we all have to learn to get along with others. Even though everyone in the company is working toward a common goal, flare-ups can still arise.

We're all human and we all have our bad days. Maybe you are having an off day because you didn't get enough sleep, or you had a big fight with your partner. Maybe your coworker isn't fully present because she's worried about her mother's health. Everyone brings key strengths and challenges into work every day.

With the help of the Enneagram, you'll be able to work in harmony with less drama. The Enneagram provides tips on how to properly communicate with your coworkers, how to resolve a workplace conflict with any of the nine Types, and how to set fair and healthy expectations for your colleagues.

Looking Ahead

By now, you have a pretty good idea of how the Enneagram system can help you with your journey into self-development, and how it can provide deeper insight into your relationships with others. The Enneagram is an incredibly complex and multifaceted personality system, but the great news is, we've already covered the essentials. You've learned what happens when the Types are stressed and when they are at the top of their game. Mostly importantly, you've discovered how the Enneagram can help foster self-awareness, mindfulness, and compassion for yourself and for the people in your life.

If you have taken the Enneagram quiz, you probably have a better idea of what Type you are. Or maybe you know what yours is and you've given the quiz to a friend or partner. Either way, you're ready to take a more in-depth look at all nine Enneagram Types. After that, in Chapters 4, 5, and 6, you can examine your Type alongside other Types you encounter. The pairings are in numerical order, so simply look for the lowest number first.

3

The Nine Enneatypes

What Enneagram Types Can Show You

In this chapter, we will dive deeply into each of the Enneagram Types, exploring their core motivations, deepest fears, and longings. You'll be able to see the people in your life through an entirely new lens. This lens will tell you how to get along with the people in your life on a whole new level. You will learn how to effectively communicate with your significant other and how to approach and handle conflict with the closest people in your life. You'll also see connections among the Types, which are shown by the Lines of Security and Stress. As you explore the different combinations and how they get along, keep in mind that a healthy and happy relationship ultimately begins within you. It's only when you love yourself that you can wholeheartedly love others.

Should You Try to Determine Someone Else's Type?

Discovering your own Type is a very personal journey. You might figure it out right away or it could take years. If determining your own Type is that difficult, you can imagine the potential issues when trying to figure out someone else's Type. Trying to Type someone else is definitely something you want to avoid. Someone can exhibit certain behaviors that might have you thinking that they're a certain Type, but only they will know what is motivating their behaviors, not you or anyone else. If you try to Type other people, there's a significant possibility that you'll get it wrong, which is a disservice to both of you. Instead, if you're interested in what Type someone might be, introduce them to the Enneagram and invite them to take the quiz earlier in this book and share the results with you!

TYPE ONE
The Reformer

KEY DESIRES Ones want to be virtuous, ideals-driven, and accurate, and do things the way they believe they should be done.

KEY FEARS Ones fear being bad, wrong, and/or corrupt, or being condemned for doing something wrong.

CORE VALUES
- Honesty
- Principles
- Humility
- Good manners
- Holds on to their beliefs
- Cleanliness and tidiness
- Fairness

STRENGTHS
- Truthful
- Ethical
- Responsible
- Purposeful
- Organized
- Hardworking
- Practical

CHALLENGES
- Inflexible
- Perfectionist
- Overly critical
- Represses anger
- Impatient
- Resentful
- Doesn't want to accept own flaws

LINES OF SECURITY AND STRESS

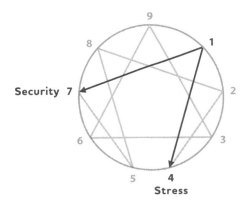

SECURITY—Ones move toward the healthy characteristics of Sevens:

- Relaxed
- Spontaneous and playful
- Less critical of themselves and others

STRESS—Ones move toward the average-to-unhealthy characteristics of Fours:

- Irrational
- Moody
- Depressed

TYPE ONE IN THE ENNEAGRAM TRIADS

Center of Intelligence—Body: Ones suppress their instinctive desires and emotions; they tend to pride themselves on how much self-control they have. They strive to maintain a certain level of perfection in order to not "lose themselves" to whims, unconscious impulses, and anger.

Hornevian Triad—Compliant Stance: Ones play by the rules and can often become workaholics and perfectionists. They do this to feel superior to others and to avoid being criticized. What they want instead of criticism is praise and recognition for being good and being right. Ones want to preserve order within their homes, jobs, and relationships. They are focused on the present and the task at hand.

Harmonic Triad—Competency Approach: Ones want to resolve conflict by holding firm to what they know to be good and true. They put their feelings and desires aside in order to remain objective in reaching a solution. Typically, conflict finds them when they are impatient, critical, or self-righteous.

Object Relations—Frustration: Ones are idealists. They are constantly looking for what is wrong and how it can be fixed. They are ardently focused on making sure they are living up to their high standards and usually expect the same from those around them. They become frustrated when people, experiences, and things are not "as they should be" (according to them), and feel a moral obligation to fix them.

WINGS

NINE WING
- Philosophical
- Emotionally reserved
- Calm
- Idealistic
- Passive
- Withdrawn
- Composed

TWO WING
- Empathetic
- Image-conscious
- Helpful
- Generous
- Tolerant
- Extroverted
- Makes connections with others

Type One with a Dominant Nine Wing

Ones with a strong Nine Wing (1w9) tend to be composed, reserved, and have a calming nature. Their emotions are less readily available, but when they do surface, they're natural and not overwhelming. 1w9s are highly idealistic, and when under stress, they can come across as condescending.

Type One with a Dominant Two Wing

Ones with a strong Two Wing (1w2) gravitate toward people and social settings. They enjoy being helpful and generous with their time and effort, but they can also be a bit self-righteous with how they expect things to be done. 1w2s can be passionate and have strong opinions.

BLIND SPOTS

Ones can have impossibly high standards. They transfer their frustration and disappointment to those around them and are unaware of how their anger presents itself in their body language.

TYPE ONE AT HOME

How to Support Them: Ones can be so hard on themselves. They have an inner critic who can be relentless at times. Be sure to acknowledge their hard work and commitment to doing the right thing.

What to Be Mindful Of: Ones can build up resentment over time when they take on too many tasks, chores, and household improvements. Suggest a family game night or a fun outdoor activity in order to relieve stress and tension.

TYPE ONE IN LOVE

Needs: Ones can be extremely self-critical. Because of this, they need people in their lives who are kind, patient, and compassionate. They also mesh well with people who value integrity and respect in all of its forms.

How to Love Them: Acknowledge Ones for all their hard work and the way they are ardently committed to doing the right thing. They feel loved when their dedication to projects, work, and self-development is acknowledged.

What to Be Grateful For: Ones are very committed to their loved one and the relationship. They want to make sure they are doing right by them and that they are living up to their own high standards of what they believe is a good partner.

TYPE ONE AT WORK

Effective Communication: Ones prefer that people be direct and kind when speaking to them. It's important to respect their opinions by listening to them and taking seriously what they have to say. They are very detail-oriented, but do not rush them when they are speaking. Be sure not to interrupt them.

Resolving Conflict: Avoid confronting Ones with criticism. It's best to take a direct but calm approach when addressing workplace concerns. They value and respect your honesty, but keep in mind they are sensitive to criticism. If their coworkers are transparent about their own mistakes, this openness creates space for Ones to admit their own faults as well. They are going to want to reach a resolution, but they must first set aside their own anger and pride.

Expectations: It's important to Ones that everyone they work with is holding up their fair share of the workload. They want tasks, assignments, and any other responsibilities to be taken seriously and to be completed on time.

TYPE TWO
The Nurturer

KEY DESIRES Twos desire to be loved and needed by others, and to feel indispensable.

KEY FEARS Twos have a fear of being unworthy of love.

CORE VALUES

- Love
- Thoughtfulness
- Focus on relationships
- Empathy for others
- Self-sacrifice
- Intimacy
- Compassion

STRENGTHS

- Generous
- Empathetic
- Warm-hearted
- Unconditional love
- Altruistic
- Helpful

CHALLENGES

- Possessive
- Codependent
- Prideful
- People-pleasing
- Intrusive
- Manipulative
- Self-serving

LINES OF SECURITY AND STRESS

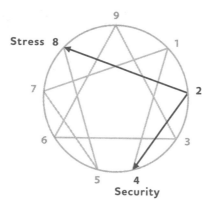

SECURITY—Twos move toward the healthy characteristics of Fours:

- Emotionally honest
- Independent from others
- Increased self-compassion

STRESS—Twos move toward the average-to-unhealthy characteristics of Eights:

- Controlling
- Aggressive
- Prideful

TYPE TWO IN THE ENNEAGRAM TRIADS

Center of Intelligence—Heart: Twos tend to be very nurturing; they want to make others feel loved and cared for. They also want to be perceived as loving and kind. They are very attuned to what others need and want, and because of this, they can create a dependency for others to need them.

Hornevian Triad—Compliant Stance: Twos crave attention; in order for them to acquire it, they will often place themselves in situations where they can be of use to people. They will be helpful, caring, and give to others in order to receive attention. They think that by providing everything someone could possibly need, it will be impossible for people to reject them.

Harmonic Triad—Positive Outlook Approach: Twos want to focus on the positive and ignore the negative. They look for the good in people and want others to see the good in them. They want the environment around them to stay light and positive as well. By doing this, no one talks or focuses on the negative aspects of what's happening or of themselves. Conflict often finds them when they avoid addressing serious issues.

Object Relations—Rejection: Twos will often reject their own needs and emotions. On a somewhat subconscious level, they don't believe that they matter enough to tend to them. They want to avoid being rejected, so they focus their attention on trying to meet the needs of others while sacrificing their own needs and wants.

WINGS

ONE WING
- Proper
- Respectful
- Flattering
- Discreet
- Self-deceptive
- Wise
- Encouraging

THREE WING
- Charming
- Ambitious
- Status-seeking
- Adaptable
- Playful
- Seductive
- Entertaining

Type Two with a Dominant One Wing

Twos with a strong One Wing (2w1) are service-oriented toward others, idealistic, and sincere. they enjoy conversation about meaningful, purposeful subjects, and are extremely empathetic when it comes to human suffering. 2w1s have high ideals and can become critical of themselves and others.

Type Two with a Dominant Three Wing

Twos with a strong Three Wing (2w3) are charmers! They're very sociable, energetic, and have a positive, can-do attitude about life. They enjoy being around others, offering support, and encouraging those around them to see the bright side of life. 2w3s can be very flirtatious and seductive, and will usually be more extroverted than 2w1s.

BLIND SPOTS

Twos can be very unaware of exactly why they want to help, nurture, and be there for others. They don't realize that they're only giving to receive. In the process of doing so much for others, they neglect themselves.

TYPE TWO AT HOME

How to Support Them: Twos are incredibly aware of everyone else's needs. Take the time to check in on them and ask how they are and how they're feeling. Instead of asking them what they need (they often don't know), do something kind for them or give them words of affirmation to let them know they are loved and cared for.

What to Be Mindful Of: Twos can be very helpful around the house and will look after younger siblings without much hesitation. Because they are so aware of who needs what, they usually take the initiative to tend to the family's needs. These behaviors can lead to feelings of resentment and a sense of entitlement due to their self-neglect.

TYPE TWO IN LOVE

Needs: Twos need plenty of alone time for a good dose of autonomy. This is so that they can separate their needs from others. Purposeful alone time helps them to look within and take care of themselves first. When they do this, they'll be able to show up full of energy for the other people in their lives.

How to Love Them: Twos like to know that their loved one is grateful to have them in their life. Whatever it is their partner wants to do for them, it should be thoughtful and just for them. They also feel loved when they are taken care of for a change.

What to Be Grateful For: Twos typically put their relationships before anything else. Their loved ones mean the world to them, and they will do almost anything to keep them healthy and thriving, and feeling loved and cared for.

TYPE TWO AT WORK

Effective Communication: Twos appreciate attentive communication. It will go a long way to be positive, encouraging, and firm (but kind) when relaying feedback. Rather than criticizing them outright, point out the value they bring to the workplace, and then share your concerns about areas where there is room for improvement.

Resolving Conflict: Resolving conflicts with Twos always goes more smoothly when they are addressed in a calm manner. It's best to invite their perspective when starting a conversation around issues. Ask Twos where they can take responsibility and how they can be helped to further their success in the company.

Expectations: Twos want to work in a positive environment and they'd prefer everyone get along so the workplace environment feels like "home." They will go out of their way to help their coworkers and managers, but they will want to be recognized for their nurturing spirit.

TYPE THREE
The Achiever

KEY DESIRES Threes desire to be valuable, wanted, and successful in whatever they do.

KEY FEARS Threes have a fear of failure and feeling worthless.

CORE VALUES
- Accomplishment
- Personal growth
- Admiration
- Reputation
- Being desired
- Recognition
- Prestige

STRENGTHS
- Ambitious
- Energetic
- Charming
- Hardworking
- Competent
- Highly driven
- Enthusiastic
- Practical

CHALLENGES
- Image-driven
- Competitive
- Out of touch with their feelings
- Always "on"
- Impatient
- Self-deceiving
- Workaholics
- Need outside validation

LINES OF SECURITY AND STRESS

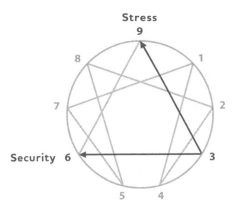

SECURITY—Threes move toward the healthy characteristics of Sixes:

- Grounded
- Responsible
- Stable

STRESS—Threes move toward the average-to-unhealthy characteristics of Nines:

- Stubborn
- Unreflective
- Apathetic

TYPE THREE IN THE ENNEAGRAM TRIADS

Center of Intelligence—Heart: Even though Threes are in the Heart Center (also known as the Feeling Center), they are disconnected from knowing their true feelings. They are so focused on what others feel and how others perceive them that they become detached from who they truly are. They have a way of projecting a successful image while not being completely truthful. They turn away from themselves and instead turn to others for validation and as a measurement of their value.

Hornevian Triad—Assertive Stance: Threes demand attention from others. They are under the impression that what they say and do is important; they expect others to not only take notice but also to praise them. If that doesn't happen, they begin to re-evaluate what their "audience" is looking for, and will adapt themselves to the image of what others want or need of them to receive attention and validation.

Harmonic Triad—Competency Approach: Threes want to resolve conflict without it affecting them or how others view them. They compartmentalize their emotions when solving a problem so that they can be as effective as possible. Conflict tends to find them when they are being competitive, disingenuous, or arrogant.

Object Relations—Attachment: Threes are continuously adapting to the expectations of others. They are fully aware of what is of high value to anyone around them because they want to maintain the attachment to their self-image as a valuable, competent, and successful person.

WINGS

TWO WING
- Vivacious
- Task-oriented
- Overly positive
- Personable
- Tactful
- Uplifting
- Tuned in to others

FOUR WING
- Imaginative
- Dynamic
- Introspective
- Pretentious
- Gracefully effective
- Self-doubting
- Creatively expressive

Type Three with a Dominant Two Wing

Threes with a strong Two Wing (3w2) are tuned in to others and are more likely to focus on the success in their relationships rather than, say, academic or professional success. They are thoughtful, personable, and enjoy being the center of attention. It can be very easy for them to alter who they are in order to be seen as popular and desirable.

Type Three with a Dominant Four Wing

Threes with a strong Four Wing (3w4) are contemplative and take a lot of pride in their work. They are wonderfully creative and enjoy expressing themselves through artistic pursuits. Dominant Four Wings can sometimes struggle between being what others want them to be and being their authentic self.

BLIND SPOTS

One of Threes' blind spots is that they find it very difficult to have conversations relating to negative issues. They will often rush through, zone out, or dismiss themselves from the discussion. They are particularly apt to behave this way when the conflict involves them having made a mistake.

TYPE THREE AT HOME

How to Support Them: Threes are usually working hard to make you feel proud of them. They want to know that you admire their efforts and are proud of what they've accomplished. This can include small-scale accomplishments (like finishing their homework or mowing the lawn) or large-scale achievements (like being promoted at work or winning an award at school). Let them know you're proud of them, and ask them how they feel about it or what it means to them.

What to Be Mindful Of: Threes are very productive, busy bees; they are always on the move with errands and other household responsibilities. They can be very hard on themselves when it comes to their work and how much they need to produce in a day. You can encourage them to slow down by inviting them to watch some TV or go for a relaxing walk with you.

TYPE THREE IN LOVE

Needs: Threes measure their worth according to outside validation. Because of this, Threes want a fair amount of attention and recognition for all that they do. What they need from their partners is the gentle and loving reminder that they are loved and admired for just being themselves.

How to Love Them: Threes generally enjoy the company of those who make them feel good about themselves. Loved ones should make an effort to spend quality time with them and enjoy each other's company. Partners can strengthen their emotional bonds with Threes by going out on a date or spending time together with friends.

What to Be Grateful For: Threes are very encouraging partners. They want you to reach your goals and tend to be supportive in your endeavors. They're usually hopeful in an enthusiastic way, which can be uplifting because you know you have someone in your corner, wishing nothing but the best for you.

TYPE THREE AT WORK

Effective Communication: Threes appreciate coworkers being very clear and concise when speaking to them; they typically speak in that same manner. If they are asked to repeat something, they may get frustrated since they tend to be impatient when under stress. Coworkers should be direct and specific when asking them for what they need.

Resolving Conflict: Threes might become defensive if they are called out about their shortcomings. They do much better if what they're doing correctly is addressed first before providing them with constructive criticism. This allows them to feel valued and gives them something to improve on. When necessary, Threes should be encouraged to speak freely about how they feel about the situation.

Expectations: Threes typically make great employees and can also excel in a leadership or managerial position. They are ambitious and strive to hit target goals; they can feel frustrated when they are interrupted. They expect to be rewarded and validated for their valiant efforts.

TYPE FOUR
The Individualist or The Romantic

KEY DESIRES Fours want to have a unique identity and a meaningful personal significance.

KEY FEARS Fours are afraid of not having an identity.

CORE VALUES
- Authenticity
- Romance
- Nonconformity
- Passion
- Self-awareness
- Originality and creativity
- Self-expression

STRENGTHS
- Self-aware
- Imaginative
- Expressive
- Highly intuitive

- Creative
- Tenderhearted

- True to themselves

CHALLENGES
- Highly sensitive
- Self-absorbed
- Temperamental
- Irrational

- Self-hating
- Envious
- Dramatic

LINES OF SECURITY AND STRESS

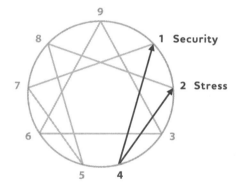

SECURITY—Fours move toward the healthy characteristics of Ones:
- Action-oriented
- Levelheaded
- Realistic

STRESS—Fours move toward the average-to-unhealthy characteristics of Twos:
- Hypochondriac
- Overbearing
- Manipulative

TYPE FOUR IN THE ENNEAGRAM TRIADS

Center of Intelligence—Heart: Fours are incredibly self-aware and in tune with their emotions. Although they crave connection to others, they often withdraw because they want to maintain a certain level of separateness from others in order to not feel ordinary. Fours in the Heart Center (also known as the Feeling Center) are focused on the uniqueness of their identity. They want to ensure that the connections they make with others are authentic and full of meaning.

Hornevian Triad—Withdrawn Stance: Fours are typically overwhelmed by the world around them. In order to protect themselves and their values, they retreat within themselves to feel closer to who they are. They feel as though they cannot meet their needs unless they can tune everything out. They are disconnected from the Body Center (also known as the Instinctual Center), making them slow to take any action.

Harmonic Triad—Reactive Approach: Fours show up to conflicts with emotional depth and they seek the same level of response. Their main concern during conflict is to be heard and understood. Conflict typically finds them when they are volatile, fickle, or self-absorbed. The pain they feel when the tension is high and they are trying to get their needs met is so intense that it feels as though they cannot contain it.

Object Relations—Frustration: Fours are idealists and can search for the ideal in their relationships. They often long for the ideal partner, their "soulmate." Reality always sets in and they begin to realize their partner has flaws, creating a chronic frustration within most (if not all) their relationships. They will also seek validation from others and will become frustrated when they are not understood.

WINGS

THREE WING

- Vivacious
- Task-oriented
- Overly positive
- Personable
- Tactful
- Uplifting
- Tuned in to others

FIVE WING

- Imaginative
- Dynamic
- Introspective
- Pretentious
- Gracefully effective
- Self-doubting
- Creatively expressive

Type Four with a Dominant Three Wing

Fours with a strong Three Wing (4w3) tend to be goal-oriented, extroverted, and social with their inner circle. Their aim is to bring their dreams to life, to realize their creative goals. They can be a bit insecure and may feel like they are constantly trying to prove their worth.

Type Four with a Dominant Five Wing

Fours with a strong Five Wing (4w5) are much more introverted and withdrawn. They prefer to be alone and struggle with being able to take action on their creative passions. They are much more cerebral and have incredibly profound insights. When it comes to romantic relationships, they sometimes find the potential heartache too much to bear.

BLIND SPOTS

One of Fours' blind spots is that they are perpetually focused on what's missing from their life. They so long for what used to be and what could possibly be that they unconsciously deprive themselves of the present moment. Because of this, they reject what they currently have, deepening their feelings of melancholy.

TYPE FOUR AT HOME

How to Support Them: Fours need to know that they are understood. If they come home from school or work feeling sad about a situation, it's best if their loved ones don't try to fix it right away; they should let them talk it out and have a good cry. Fours need others at home to just be there for them emotionally first; after they feel they've been heard, they will be ready to let them know how they can help. Fours don't like to be pushed, but eventually will let their loved ones know when they're available. Fours need to feel that there are others at home who will listen to them, validate their emotions, and refrain from giving advice unless they request it.

What to Be Mindful Of: Fours are sensitive people who can easily become overwhelmed. If there is a lot of chaos or stress happening at school or work, they need a peaceful environment to come home to so that they can recharge. They're going to want to be alone, but their loved ones should know that they'll return when they've had a chance to process everything that happened that day.

TYPE FOUR IN LOVE

Needs: In a relationship, Fours may sometimes push away their partner or pull away themselves. This is due to their fear of being abandoned. Fours need to be shown understanding and love through these times. They require empathy and reassurance from their loved one that no matter what, they'll be there when Fours are ready to return.

How to Love Them: Fours will often not have a great deal of self-worth. They feel loved when they're reminded, such as with words of affirmation or a heartfelt letter, just how much they mean to their loved one. Sending Fours a special gift can remind Fours of how much their partners sincerely love them.

What to Be Grateful For: Fours have a great well of empathy and an understanding of human suffering. They bring a beautiful intensity to their relationships and offer their hearts to you with childlike abandon. This makes Fours the most romantic Type of the Enneagram.

TYPE FOUR AT WORK

Effective Communication: Fours are typically articulate and can speak with great intensity, but they can be easily triggered when they think they are being misunderstood. Coworkers can connect with them by appreciating their creativity and by inviting them into conversations where they can share their thoughts and feelings.

Resolving Conflict: Fours can be overly emotional; during the conflict, they are highly reactive. Remain calm and even-keeled so as to not fuel their emotions. Ask them to not withdraw, and remind them that you're looking to resolve the issue at hand. Be empathetic, but remain firm so they understand what is being required of them to find a solution.

Expectations: When working alongside Fours, you can count on their wonderful creativity and emotional connection, and their need to remain autonomous. They will want to express themselves in some way with their tasks and with the relationships around them. They want to maintain a balance between their individuality and their connection to the company.

TYPE FIVE
The Observer

KEY DESIRES Fives want to be competent, autonomous, and capable.

KEY FEARS Fives fear being helpless, dependent, and incapable.

CORE VALUES
- Autonomy
- Discovery
- Knowledge
- Self-reliance
- Innovation
- Privacy
- Intellectual conversations

STRENGTHS
- Cerebral
- Insightful
- Perceptive
- Intellectual
- Objective
- Innovative
- Dependable

CHALLENGES
- Withdrawn
- Intense
- Obsessive
- Arrogant
- High-strung
- Detached
- Stingy

LINES OF SECURITY AND STRESS

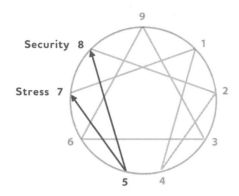

SECURITY—Fives move toward the healthy characteristics of Eights:
- Self-confident
- Openhearted
- Assertive

STRESS—Fives move toward the average-to-unhealthy characteristics of Sevens:
- Insensitive
- Unreliable
- Scattered

TYPE FIVE IN THE ENNEAGRAM TRIADS

Center of Intelligence—Head: Fives, as their nickname suggests, are the observers of the Enneagram. They prefer to remain on the outside looking in, as it allows them to feel safe. Away from people, their emotional, mental, and physical resources will not be taxed. Once they feel comfortable and confident, they'll join the world. However, what usually ends up happening is that every question Fives answer invites another question, making them retreat back into their mind, where they feel secure.

Hornevian Triad—Withdrawn Stance: Fives can feel unsafe in the world—they might even view it as threatening. When this happens, they withdraw to feel secure and begin to minimize their dependency on people and material things. They spend a lot of time in their minds and studying topics they want to master in order to better understand how the world works.

Harmonic Triad—Competency Approach: Fives believe that conflict can only be solved by fully understanding the problem and finding the best solution. They don't care for arguments because they carry too much emotion, so they push away all emotion in order to remain competent. Conflict usually finds them when they are too detached or find it difficult to recognize other people's emotions.

Object Relations—Rejection: Fives fear rejection, so in order to protect their emotional needs, they begin to deny themselves connection to others. Fives tend to rely solely on their intelligence to connect to others. They strive to become intellectually resourceful so that others may come to them and appreciate them for it. They think that if they remove emotion from their relationships, they won't ever be emotionally rejected.

WINGS

FOUR WING
- Imaginative
- Curious
- Original
- Hypersensitive
- Introspective
- Afraid of intimacy
- Open-minded

SIX WING
- Philosophical
- Objective
- Disciplined
- Suspicious
- Cooperative
- Scientific
- Emotionally reserved

Type Five with a Dominant Four Wing

Fives with a strong Four Wing (5w4) love to create what hasn't yet been formulated or manifested. They enjoy expressing their imagination through abstract art and original ideas. They are quite independent and their emotions are deep and intense. They can become locked into their heart and their mind, with very little connection to their physical body.

Type Five with a Dominant Six Wing

Fives with a strong Six Wing (5w6) tend to be logical and organized. They are practical and usually work in a profession that involves solving problems and allows them to use their observation skills. They're generally less emotional than 5w4s, but can become suspicious of other people's motives. They can also lack social skills.

BLIND SPOTS

Fives usually have vast knowledge on various topics and can unknowingly come across as arrogant or snobby. This can cause people around them to shut down and creates a barrier for people to connect with Fives. They often lack the awareness of how others are relating to them and might feel rejected by those who can't keep up with their intellect.

TYPE FIVE AT HOME

How to Support Them: Fives need a great deal of alone time to process, recharge, and protect their energies. This can sometimes feel like rejection to other members of the family. It helps to have open communication with Fives; they prefer their loved ones to be direct with them. When Fives go to their room and shut the door, others in the household should not assume they are being rejected; they can ask if Fives need time alone.

What to Be Mindful Of: Fives can get very focused on doing projects around the house. They can spend hours upon hours researching how to fix the bathroom sink or trying to figure out the solution to a math equation. Because of their intense focus, they can neglect their personal hygiene. Loved ones can kindly remind them to get some fresh air, exercise, or take a shower.

TYPE FIVE IN LOVE

Needs: When Fives choose to be in a relationship, their loved one can trust that they are very important to them and that they truly enjoy their company. However, Fives still require a fair amount of alone time. Their partner should recognize that Fives' need to be alone is not something to be taken personally. Fives will feel loved and cared for if they're allowed to have this time to themselves without guilt.

How to Love Them: Fives value their autonomy and enjoy being with people who don't require a lot of emotional connection. They are attracted to people who are also independent, like them, and share similar interests. A great way to connect with Fives is to pick a topic they genuinely love and dive deep into the details. They'll love that!

What to Be Grateful For: Fives are thoughtful and have a great deal of logic. They typically stay very objective and calm in a crisis, and they'll never push you to do anything you don't want to. There's a lot to be valued about someone who will respect your boundaries.

TYPE FIVE AT WORK

Effective Communication: Fives are usually respectful in their communication and behavior. They are nonintrusive but can be highstrung at times. They are typically emotionally detached when they speak and prefer the same style when spoken to. Allow them plenty of personal space to process and don't create an environment where an emotional response is required of them (e.g., throwing them a surprise birthday party or giving them a gift in front of a crowd).

Resolving Conflict: Fives prefer that others be direct with them and supply them with all the information necessary to accurately assess the situation. Adding emotions to the equation should be avoided, unless it's a personal issue and can't be sidestepped. In that case, they might need a longer period of time to process the issue and most likely will be unable to give an immediate response.

Expectations: Fives prefer to work alone but can also benefit from some level of interpersonal interactions. Though they may seem closed off or isolated, be patient; eventually they'll come out of their shell from time to time. What's wonderful is, when they do, what they have to say is typically brilliant or insightful.

TYPE SIX
The Loyal Skeptic

KEY DESIRES Sixes want support and security.

KEY FEARS Sixes fear being without guidance and support.

CORE VALUES
- Community
- Saving money
- Commitment
- Security
- Faithfulness
- Stability
- Collaboration

STRENGTHS
- Reliable
- Trustworthy
- Loyal
- Courageous
- Observant
- Witty
- Perceptive

CHALLENGES

- Anxious
- Pessimistic
- Defensive
- Reactive
- Suspicious
- Contradictory
- Hypervigilant

LINES OF SECURITY AND STRESS

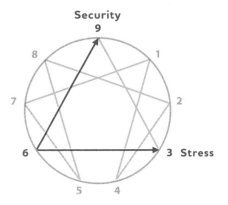

SECURITY—Sixes move toward the healthy characteristics of Nines:

- Optimistic
- Calm
- Adaptive

STRESS—Sixes move toward the average-to-unhealthy characteristics of Threes:

- Terrified of failure
- Arrogant
- Opportunistic

TYPE SIX IN THE ENNEAGRAM TRIADS

Center of Intelligence—Head: Sixes are out of touch with their inner guidance. They doubt their own abilities and can have serious anxiety over making decisions. They seek reassurance from other people in order to feel supported and affirmed. Every so often, though, the anxious Six will take a leap of faith and confront authority.

Hornevian Triad—Compliant Stance: Sixes typically follow the rules to feel secure. They think that if they properly abide by them and continue to be loyal to authority figures, their security will be guaranteed. When Sixes don't receive the security and support they so deeply crave from authority figures, they will try even harder to commit, or will begin to rebel and look for security elsewhere.

Harmonic Triad—Reactive Approach: Sixes battle with anxiety in general but conflict increases its intensity, making them highly sensitive and reactive. They want to be strong and stand their ground, but at the same time, they don't want to lose the support of those around them. Conflict usually finds them when they are anxious, indecisive, or untrusting.

Object Relations—Attachment: Sixes don't believe in themselves enough to trust their own instincts, opinions, or ideas. They will often seek that from an authority figure or from an institution. Sixes acquire their sense of self through the attachment they have with the important people in their lives or the system with which they associate, such as their religion.

WINGS

FIVE WING
- Idiosyncratic
- Problem-solvers
- Extremely vigilant
- Quiet
- Conservative
- Focused
- Cynical

SEVEN WING
- Social
- Fun-loving
- Impulsive
- Charmingly funny

- Extroverted
- Want to be liked

- Self-deprecating

Type Six with a Dominant Five Wing

Sixes with a strong Five Wing (6w5) are comfortable living in their inner world. They enjoy learning, problem-solving, and mastering skills. They typically have a great deal of focus and a sense of independence, and are less likely to seek out the advice of their friends. If they become overwhelmed, they tend to become reclusive and struggle to take action.

Type Six with a Dominant Seven Wing

Sixes with a strong Seven Wing (6w7) are comfortable in the outer world, as the Seven Wing seeks security through a variety of experiences and can strongly influence Sixes with spontaneity. They will likely be a bit more extroverted and active than 6w5s. They might struggle with discipline and become dependent on the advice of friends and confidants.

BLIND SPOTS

Sixes devote a great deal of their time and energy to all the things that can go wrong. This habitual approach to life can look like negative behavior to others. Sixes are unable to identify this cycle for themselves. If their pessimism is pointed out, Sixes may descend into a psychological cycle of doubt, anxiousness, and avoidance.

TYPE SIX AT HOME

How to Support Them: Sixes require a great deal of security and support, especially from their family members. This is where Sixes begin to establish a respect for authority and where they feel supported by those who love and know them the best. When loved ones are consistent with what they say they're going to do, Sixes will feel more trusting, safe, and secure.

What to Be Mindful Of: Sixes carry a lot of anxiety with them; they worry about all the many things that could go wrong. If they have a test coming up, they might fret for weeks about it; if they are up for a promotion, they might become highly reactive and agitated on the days leading up to the decision. The stress and the thrill of the anticipated moment is often not worth the anxiety leading up to it. Others at home should give them extra love and support during especially difficult times. They should keep things positive but also be open to listening to their worries and grievances.

TYPE SIX IN LOVE

Needs: Most people involved in loving relationships will have different opinions from time to time, but Sixes need to know that even though they and their loved one may not see eye to eye on something, that person still loves and cares about them. They need to be reminded that it's okay to express opposing points of view as long as there is mutual respect for them. In a supportive, nonjudgmental environment, Sixes can feel relaxed and optimistic about being in the relationship.

How to Love Them: Sixes need to be listened to when they are anxious and seeking some extra reassurance that everything is going to be okay. Their loved one should hold space for their anxieties without judging them. Then, when the time is right, they can both joke and laugh to lighten the mood and their hearts.

What to Be Grateful For: Sixes are known for being incredibly loyal and warm, and they are wholeheartedly committed to their relationships. Whoever they love will have someone in their life who will stick with them through thick and thin. They are very supportive partners who want a partner who will stay just as loyal to them.

TYPE SIX AT WORK

Effective Communication: Coworkers need to tell Sixes exactly what is expected of them concerning their tasks and responsibilities. Although Sixes are tentative, they are friendly and engaging when they speak. They can carry quite a bit of nervous energy if they are in an environment that they feel unsure about. They tend to cover up these feelings of insecurity with either self-deprecating humor, sweet candor, or a rebellious attitude. When Sixes feel confident, they can dive deeper into more serious conversations and enjoy playing devil's advocate. Sixes respond well if their attention to detail and problem-solving are appreciated.

Resolving Conflict: When approaching Sixes to resolve conflict, it's best to avoid any ambiguity. Everything needs to be laid out for them and they should be given time to ask questions to find clarity. If they resist taking responsibility for something they've done, it is best that coworkers insist that Sixes explain their point of view. This could test them—but Sixes tend to test others when they feel threatened in some way.

Expectations: Sixes have amazing perception and call on their intellect to figure out the world around them. They need rules, guidelines, and clear boundaries in order to feel secure at their job. If there is too much ambiguity in the workplace, they may procrastinate and put off their duties. When Sixes reach out for reassurance during such times, they should be encouraged to trust their instincts.

TYPE SEVEN
The Enthusiast

KEY DESIRES Sevens desire freedom, contentment, and having their needs fulfilled.

KEY FEARS Sevens fear being in emotional, physical, or mental pain, or being deprived.

CORE VALUES

- Pleasure
- Independence
- Friendships
- Having enjoyable opportunities
- Having a variety of experiences
- Optimism
- Sense of adventure

STRENGTHS

- Foresighted
- Energetic
- Quick-thinking
- Spontaneous
- Practical
- Flexible
- Enthusiastic

CHALLENGES

- Impulsive
- Irresponsible
- Unrealistic
- Impatient
- Scattered
- Insensitive
- Undisciplined

LINES OF SECURITY AND STRESS

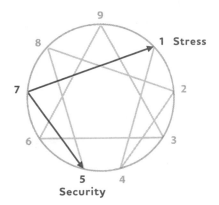

SECURITY—Sevens move toward the healthy characteristics of Fives:

- Observant
- Intentional
- Able to sit with their uncomfortable emotions

STRESS—Sevens move toward the average-to-unhealthy characteristics of Ones:

- Perfectionistic
- Overly critical
- Self-righteous

TYPE SEVEN IN THE ENNEAGRAM TRIADS

Center of Intelligence—Head: Sevens usually don't realize that they are afraid of their inner world. They try to avoid feelings of sadness, grief, and shame by taking action and staying perpetually preoccupied with the outside world. This keeps feelings of anxiety (or any other negative emotions) at bay. They are seeking security, but they're not quite sure how to attain it, so they spend a great deal of time pursuing that elusive peace of mind with a variety of experiences. They don't commit to one thing in case something better presents itself.

Hornevian Triad—Assertive Stance: Sevens seek fulfillment in a variety of forms. This comes from the need to quell their anxieties with movement, action, and activities that bring them pleasure. They may demand or even feel entitled that others provide these experiences and possibilities for them. If Sevens don't feel fulfilled, they'll quickly seek it elsewhere. When others can't provide them with the contentment they are constantly seeking, they'll move on and satisfy their needs in some other way.

Harmonic Triad—Positive Outlook Approach: Sevens have a positive outlook on life. They tend to focus on the good that could happen or the good in people. They tend to gloss over conflict as they'd rather spend their energy focusing on the positives and moving forward. During times of conflict, they think it's important to look on the bright side and try to find better alternatives. Conflict usually finds them when they are impatient, unrealistic, or irresponsible.

Object Relations—Frustration: Since Sevens are in pursuit of contentment and ideal scenarios where they feel safe, they become frustrated when the situation they are in (or the people they are with) is not quite how they imagined it would be. This frustration pulls them out of the present moment to contemplate future experiences that have the potential to be "amazing!"

WINGS

SIX WING
- Witty
- Joie de vivre
- Engaging
- Fickle
- Lighthearted
- Apprehensive
- Dependable

EIGHT WING
- Gregarious
- Independent
- Excessive
- Dutiful

- Boisterous
- Impatient

- Can-do attitude

Type Seven with a Dominant Six Wing

Sevens with a strong Six Wing (7w6) are eager to learn, enthusiastic, and very adventurous. They still seek out a variety of new experiences, but tend to stick to commitments and promises they've made. 7w6s have a major fear of missing out and have a difficult time determining which plan to follow.

Type Seven with a Dominant Eight Wing

Sevens with a strong Eight Wing (7w8) possess leadership qualities. They have great self-confidence and endurance, and they seek out opportunities. They do have a fear of missing out, but it's typically not as strong at that of 7w6s. They truly enjoy being in the company of their friends and will usually avoid situations where they are deprived of pleasure or controlled.

BLIND SPOTS

Sevens can digest and understand context fairly quickly, but sometimes won't grasp the full extent of a situation before prematurely jumping into action. They might proclaim to have an expertise when they really don't understand the depths of the matter. This can look misleading to people, who may question their capabilities.

TYPE SEVEN AT HOME

How to Support Them: Sevens can get bored more quickly than other Types. They may passionately love a certain toy or activity, but, within hours, will lose interest in it. This can also be an adult who has a new hobby every week. For children who are Sevens, it's important to remind them that stillness is okay—they don't always have to be doing something. Quiet time alone could be beneficial to them. For adult Sevens, it helps to check in with them to see if they're avoiding something painful by jumping from project to project.

What to Be Mindful Of: Sevens tend to avoid pain, but it is critical for healthy development and healthy relationships to process darker emotions. Sevens need help developing a healthy framework for addressing their worries, pain, and anxieties without feeling overwhelmed with their own or others' emotions.

TYPE SEVEN IN LOVE

Needs: Sevens need a partner who will be flexible (like them), spontaneous, and fun-loving. This will have the Seven feeling as if they've found their soulmate. However, they also need to be reminded to slow down their impulses every once in a while. They are pretty independent but do enjoy being in the company of their partner. Quality time is usually this Type's "love language."

How to Love Them: Ultimately, Sevens want companionship, love, and freedom. They enjoy having stimulating conversations and planning adventures. They don't like to be told what to do or to be limited in any way. Usually, they are so focused on the future of things that they appreciate the reminder to enjoy and savor the present moment.

What to Be Grateful For: Sevens bring energy, vitality, and joy to a relationship. They remind their partners just how much fun life can be. It can feel wonderfully invigorating to be in their presence. They bring with them a healthy dose of optimism that allows others to eventually recognize that no matter how difficult things get, life goes on, and it's going to be great.

TYPE SEVEN AT WORK

Effective Communication: Sevens have a friendly and positive disposition, so their communication is usually the same, with a sprinkle of lighthearted wit and excitement. They tend to respond better if the communication matches their light, friendly style. Remain upbeat and avoid getting too negative.

Resolving Conflict: Resolving conflict with Sevens can get a little tricky if they are not open to taking responsibility. This conversation will fare better if it's done privately and away from distractions. It's best for the person in a position of leadership to be firm, stay on track, and not let Sevens know the desired resolution. Sevens can use a kind push to talk about their own grievances, and will ultimately come up with several solutions on their own.

Expectations: Sevens thrive in active, stimulating, and creative environments. They want to be able to exercise their creative thinking and have as much flexibility as possible. They are energized and inspired by new ideas and a variety of tasks. They might feel limited or stressed if they don't have enough social interaction, or if they are kept doing the same assignments day after day.

TYPE EIGHT
The Protector

KEY DESIRES Eights want to be self-reliant and able to control their situation.
KEY FEARS Eights fear being harmed, controlled, or manipulated by others.

CORE VALUES

- Respect
- Directness
- Courage
- Boldness

- Love and passion
- Championing for others
- Protecting self and others

STRENGTHS

- Assertive
- Protective
- Independent
- Leadership
- Influential
- Generous
- Vitality

CHALLENGES

- Vulnerability
- Controlling
- Quick to anger
- Intimidating
- Confrontational
- Excessiveness
- Dominating

LINES OF SECURITY AND STRESS

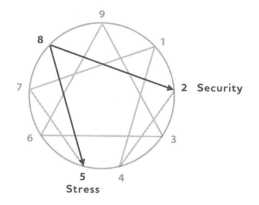

SECURITY—Eights move toward the healthy characteristics of Twos:

- Compassionate
- Vulnerable
- Sincere

STRESS—Eights move toward the average-to-unhealthy characteristics of Fives:

- Cynical
- Fearful
- Isolated

TYPE EIGHT IN THE ENNEAGRAM TRIADS

Center of Intelligence—Body: Eights have a very strong connection to their instincts and they tend to overexpress them. They're usually pretty quick to react or respond to any signal from the body, such as gut instincts or strong and powerful impulses. They are always trying to remain in control and on guard. This is due to the fact that they need to feel as though they are invincible and can handle anything that is thrown at them. They loathe feeling vulnerable but become much more relaxed and at peace when they finally allow themselves to open their hearts to others.

Hornevian Triad—Assertive Stance: Eights are striving for autonomy and will go to whatever means necessary in order to achieve it, even if that entails physically pushing themselves through. They want to be able to take charge, make decisions, and sometimes gain power. It's when they lose that sense of control that they can become aggressive and confrontational, and battle anyone in authority. They can sometimes come across to the other Types as blunt and tactless; more than anything, Eights are usually trying their best to quickly resolve a difficult situation.

Harmonic Triad—Reactive Approach: Eights tend to be easily angered. It's difficult for them to censor themselves during conflict because they have very strong and demanding impulses, and they don't have any issue confronting things head-on. Conflict finds them when they are confrontational, controlling, or domineering.

Object Relations—Rejection: Eights don't want to feel vulnerable. When it comes to their communicating their needs, they will often reject help because to them accepting it is showing weakness. Instead, they want others to see them as pillars of strength. They want to be the more powerful and resourceful ones in the room.

WINGS

SEVEN WING

- Visionary
- High mental energy
- Entrepreneurial
- Assertive

- Power-seeking
- Charismatic
- Combative

NINE WING

- Leader
- Benevolent
- Well-liked
- Patient

- Gentle and strong
- Stubborn
- Bottles up emotions

Type Eight with a Dominant Seven Wing

Eights with a strong Seven Wing (8w7) are self-confident, love to be around people, and are practical when it comes to making decisions and their behavior. The fear of being controlled is stronger with 8w7s than with 8w9. They're likely to have a cheerful disposition and a charismatic wit. On the challenging side, they can be impatient, workaholic, and highly impulsive.

Type Eight with a Dominant Nine Wing

Eights with a strong Nine Wing (8w9) have a laid back and relaxed way about them. They're less intimidating than 8w7s but usually prefer to be in leadership positions to avoid being controlled. They tend to be reluctant to open up emotionally and can spend a great deal of time building emotional walls. They are naturally confident but do struggle with emotional detachment.

BLIND SPOTS

Eights don't realize how strong and intimidating their energy and presence can be. They are so focused on the result they are trying to achieve that they dismiss others in the interim or make them feel as though their personal space is being invaded. During this time, Eights are unaware of how their behavior is affecting others.

TYPE EIGHT AT HOME

How to Support Them: One of the best ways to support Eights at home is to understand them and where they're coming from. They tend to take on a lot of stress, but they're not great at talking about their emotions, so it's important to check in on them. They prefer that loved ones are direct with them and prefer that they not make them feel weak. Even having a casual conversation with them will create space for them to open up. They do feel things deeply, but refrain from showing it, as it feels like weakness to them. So, if they do cry, their loved ones should not make a big deal about it and just let them know they are supported.

What to Be Mindful Of: Eights are outspoken and don't like to be told what to do. They typically have great instincts and act on them almost instantly. This behavior can escalate quickly when they take on a great amount of responsibility. If they are the adult in the home, they're probably "in charge." If they're a child in the home, they probably act older than their age and might be taking on more than they should. Loved ones at home should take notice if this is happening and check in with Eights to see if there is anything that can be done as a family to lighten their load.

TYPE EIGHT IN LOVE

Needs: Eights value strength. They want a partner who is going to be there through thick and thin, who knows how to get things done with little to no direction. They feel best with someone who can stand up for themselves and for them. They need to know that they can trust and rely on their partner.

How to Love Them: Type Eights appear to be pillars of strength and for the most part, it's true. However, deep down, they do have a tender heart. To truly love them, it's important that partners not just acknowledge and respect their exterior but value and get to know and understand what's underneath Eights' layers. They want to share their heart with someone they can trust who can handle it.

What to Be Grateful For: Eights will give their loved one their loyalty, trust, and heart once they know they can trust them. It might take a while, but once their loved one has earned a place within their protective space, they will realize the great lengths that Eights are willing to go for them.

TYPE EIGHT AT WORK

Effective Communication: Eights are direct, honest, and up-front, and prefer others treat them the same way. Avoid ambiguity or any overly emotional language. They'll be put off and confused that perhaps you're trying to manipulate them. Making eye contact with them is always a must.

Resolving Conflict: Resolving conflict with Eights will take some patience and strategy. They usually have no issues with confrontation and are ready to go when the situation presents itself. If you are a supervisor trying to resolve an issue, it's important to stand your ground and not back down in the presence of their strength. You can meet them at their level of energy but maintain balance so they don't get carried away. Be firm but empathize with any feelings they reveal.

Expectations: Eights work best in an environment where they have their independence and people report to them. Most Eights would thrive in a supervisory or managerial position. This allows them to exercise their strengths. They have an abundance of energy and enjoy working at a fast speed. They feel encouraged when asked their opinion and when others look up to them as a leader.

TYPE NINE
The Mediator

KEY DESIRES Nines desire inner peace and stability.

KEY FEARS Nines fear conflict, and both inner and outer chaos.

CORE VALUES
- Peace of mind
- Creativity
- Empathy
- Kindness and generosity
- Companionship
- Acceptance
- Relaxation

STRENGTHS
- Patient
- Optimistic
- Easygoing
- Agreeable
- Understanding
- Genuine
- Supportive

CHALLENGES
- Stagnant
- Too conciliatory
- Passive-aggressive
- Conflict-avoidant
- Stubborn
- Indecisive
- Averse to change

LINES OF SECURITY AND STRESS

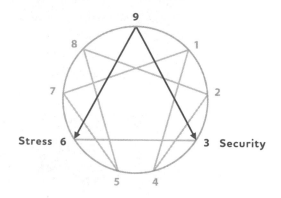

SECURITY—Nines move toward the healthy characteristics of Threes:

- Self-assured
- Highly efficient
- Focused and energetic

STRESS—Nines move toward the average-to-unhealthy characteristics of Sixes:

- Anxious
- Self-doubting
- Pessimistic

TYPE NINE IN THE ENNEAGRAM TRIADS

Center of Intelligence—Body: Nines are disconnected from their instincts. They're unsure about asserting themselves, and afraid that it will cause inner and outer conflict. This creates a cycle for them that begins with them shutting down most of their natural instincts. They're trying to hold onto their autonomy by not making decisions and opposing change. If, for whatever reason, they don't get the space and peace they're looking for, their repressed anger will come out in passive-aggressive behavior.

Hornevian Triad—Withdrawn Stance: Nines essentially want control over their autonomy, and to achieve this, they withdraw from change. This gives them a sense of peace and comfort. They use the same tactic to minimize their desires. They prefer comfort and routine over change and progress. They can spend a great deal of time fantasizing and idealizing their worlds, yet they prefer to remain in an idealized state as opposed to actual reality. They have a difficult time speaking up for themselves and expressing their needs.

Harmonic Triad—Positive Outlook Approach: Nines focus their attention on the positive side of their relationships and their environment. They are extremely conflict-avoidant and will deny and avoid problematic issues at great cost. This strengthens their attachment to denial. Having a positive outlook brings the Nine a great deal of peace and gives them a relatively calm and soothing demeanor. However, the downside is that denying reality makes it difficult to improve situations or find solutions to challenges. By avoiding conflict, they find themselves in the very place they try so hard to avoid.

Object Relations—Attachment: Nines want to remain in a calm and steady flow. They feel best when they are maintaining their chosen internal state. In order to keep the status quo going, they adapt to their environment and the people within it. They would much rather attach themselves to the decisions that other people make in order to avoid conflict or disruption of their world.

WINGS

EIGHT WING

- Caring leaders
- Independent
- Stubborn
- Generous
- Self-motivated
- Defensive
- Strong willpower

ONE WING

- Peaceful
- Highly principled
- Composed
- Sarcastic

- Discerning
- Self-critical
- Modest

Type Nine with a Dominant Eight Wing

Nines with a strong Eight Wing (9w8) tend to struggle internally with opposing motivations. At their core, they want to avoid conflict, but their Eight Wing encourages them to confront the conflict head-on. They're more outgoing and adventurous than 9w1s. They have a tendency to oscillate between wanting to keep the peace, and becoming more assertive and standing up for themselves. This usually only happens when they've become angered.

Type Nine with a Dominant One Wing

Nines with a strong One Wing (9w1) thrive with routine and prefer a peaceful environment. Their main objective most of the time is to maintain peace internally and externally. They don't want to deal with negative emotions and can become quite avoidant of anything that threatens this mission. They typically see many sides to a situation, and though they want to help, they'll hold back from getting involved if their needs are going to be affected.

BLIND SPOTS

Type Nines have trouble identifying conflict and situations that need to be addressed. They will try to minimize the issues and avoid getting upset—but in so doing, they're continuing to repress their anger and desires. They need to build their self-awareness and begin to accept that conflict is a natural part of life. It doesn't have to be frightening, and it can even be beneficial to their overall mission of wanting to have peace.

TYPE NINE AT HOME

How to Support Them: The most important piece of the puzzle when it comes to living with Nines is to recognize that they are not going to speak up when they have a need, want, or even a strong desire. They need to be asked their opinions, and when they're asked, it's vital that they are not rushed or pressured in any way. Loved ones should check in with them and ask them a few questions every day to let them know they're interested in and value what Nines have to say.

What to Be Mindful Of: Nines tend to have low energy. This can look like laziness, but it goes deeper than that. They try to not let things bother them, which can be a positive trait. During times of heightened stress or sadness, however, they can begin to forget their own needs. This is when you'll need to kindly intervene. If it's a child, make sure everything is okay at school and among their friendships. If you have an adult Nine in the home who begins to lose interest in taking care of themselves, sit down and talk about what's going on at work or if they're struggling internally.

TYPE NINE IN LOVE

Needs: Nines value equanimity. They want a partner who is going to be accepting, loving, and compassionate. They do well with someone who can encourage them and not pressure them. They need a good amount of affirming and a partner who allows them to feel safe when they need to stand up for themselves.

How to Love Them: Nines spend a great deal of their time focusing on others. They are happy to let you make both small decisions (such as picking where you're going to eat or choosing the movie you're going to watch) and large decisions as well. One of the best ways to love them is to switch the focus onto them—but don't force it. It will get easier over time for them to realize that you truly do care and value their opinion.

What to Be Grateful For: Nines have incredible patience and understanding for everyone, but when it comes to those they love and respect, it goes above and beyond. They are beautiful souls who are truly aiming to please and adapt to their partners. It's crucial to not walk all over them or to take advantage of their mild-mannered spirit. They are incredibly empathetic and deserving of the same love they give.

TYPE NINE AT WORK

Effective Communication: Nines are calm and collected when they talk. They usually take longer getting around to exactly what they want to say. Avoid rushing them to get to their point, which will only cause them to shut down. Learn to be patient with them and don't come on too strong. They will get to the point and when they do, it's usually pretty profound and poignant. They enjoy being involved in group discussion and having their opinions asked of them. Just remember to give them the time they need to express themselves.

Resolving Conflict: To resolve a disagreement with Nines, coworkers need to keep in mind that they value fairness and justice, but they are also quite conflict-avoidant. They usually withdraw from fear of being overwhelmed with the conflict. Talk to them calmly and let them know ahead of time (before entering into the heated discussion) that you are looking for a solution to a certain problem. This lets their brain calm down. When presenting your side of the argument, remain composed and ask them what they need.

Expectations: Nines are usually very down-to-earth and can be great to work with, as they value inclusivity and enjoy being a part of a team. They are adaptable, agreeable, and, because they seek a peaceful environment, they rarely cause conflict. They do have a tendency to be stubborn or ambivalent under stress.

4

Using the Enneagram to Improve Relationships at Home

TYPE ONE & TYPE ONE

STRENGTHS
- Thrive in a clean environment
- Enjoy having routines
- Value time together

CHALLENGES
- Overly high expectations
- Power struggles
- Difficulty letting go

LIVING IN HARMONY

At home, Ones value keeping an orderly home, maintaining self-discipline, and being fair to each other. They typically have traditional family values as well as wholesome integrity, which brings them to a deep understanding of each other. They know that they can rely on each other and will always try their best to keep their promises. They also strive to uphold their social responsibilities, like recycling and volunteering in their community. Because they are usually conscious of their spending, they tend to enjoy thrifting. Ones' personal values are usually reflected in their home.

CHALLENGES

Ones can have difficulty expressing how they feel and usually communicate their anger through sarcasm and frustration. This will usually come across in passive-aggressive ways. If both Ones are angry with each other, it's usually due to one of them not meeting certain household standards, being sloppy, or simply needing to be right. They both have difficulty letting go and moving on.

CONFLICT RESOLUTION

It's important for Ones who are living together to not just understand the household rules but to agree to them. This will make it easier when a difference of opinion arises. Both of them should practice compassion when the other makes mistakes and resist the urge to criticize or correct them. This will help both of them have more compassion for themselves and others—and they'll feel loved rather than judged. It's also important that they spend quality time together, such as doing something together as a family.

TYPE ONE & TYPE TWO

STRENGTHS
- Desire a clean and cozy household
- Enjoy lighthearted activities together
- Understand each other's values

CHALLENGES
- Resentment builds easily
- Hold in their frustrations
- Arguments can be explosive

LIVING IN HARMONY

Ones and Twos coexist at home pretty well together. Ones shape and uphold the values of the household, which are integrity, rules, and manners. Twos, on the other hand, use their loving and nurturing nature to support and care for those they love. Both these Types usually enjoy keeping a tidy space, hosting guests, and creating a warm and welcoming atmosphere in their home.

CHALLENGES

In a family dynamic, Ones are either hard workers or diligent students who need praise and positive affirmation to keep up their spirits and soften their mood. Twos, on the other hand, are quite relational and good at managing their emotions. They value their relationships, so you will often find them helping and looking for ways in which they are needed by others in the home. Problems can arise when Twos start to feel unloved because they are not getting their needs met.

CONFLICT RESOLUTION

It's crucial that Ones understand that Twos need more emotional connection than they do. They can improve their relationship by being attentive when Twos speak, spending quality time with them, and asking them how their day has been. Twos should avoid becoming overly emotional when approaching Ones. They should also be mindful of keeping things organized and tidy at home, which helps make Ones feel appreciated.

TYPE ONE & TYPE THREE

STRENGTHS
- Want their home to represent who they are
- Consistent with schedules
- Value household contribution

CHALLENGES
- Spend too much time working
- Perfectionism and vanity
- Don't talk about emotions

LIVING IN HARMONY

Ones and Threes at home are service- and goal-oriented. They both are full of energy, which they focus on doing household tasks or planning family dinners and vacations. They both know how to manage and sustain an efficient and successful household. Ones makes sure everyone is contributing to household chores; Threes make sure homework gets done and kids make it to their extracurricular activities. Threes value Ones' precision and competence in making home improvements or working on personal projects. They find it motivating that Ones exceed their expectations in terms of quality and attention to detail. Ones are focused on self-improvement and home improvements, and they usually feel supported by Threes' encouragement and inspiration.

CHALLENGES

Issues arise when Threes begin to feel Ones are being too critical or when Ones become frustrated with what they perceive as Threes' self-involvement. They both have a difficult time expressing their emotions and will struggle with the need to be respected and admired by the other because both are reticent and aren't accustomed to giving praise.

CONFLICT RESOLUTION

Both Types are pragmatic and logical, but they lack emotional depth. It's vital to practice showing each other where they're coming from on an emotional level. Spend time together at home, opening up to each other. It might be difficult at first, but they can always set a timer and allow ten to fifteen minutes for each to share what might be bothering them. It's important to actively listen while the other speaks and to give each other an equal amount of time to express themselves. Over time, the practice will foster more compassion and strengthen the bond between Ones and Threes.

TYPE ONE & TYPE FOUR

STRENGTHS
- Value integrity and honesty
- Take interest in self-improvement
- Enjoy being in a beautiful surrounding

CHALLENGES
- Sensitive to criticism
- Easily discouraged
- Trouble letting go

LIVING IN HARMONY

Ones and Fours complement each other well at home. They have a desire for integrity and both live for a higher purpose. They both admire each other's idealism and need for a happy and loving home. Together, they bring a balance of action and feeling. Because they both have a strong interest in self-development, they can be a great support to one another. When this duo works together toward a common goal, they can improve the atmosphere and efficiency of the household.

CHALLENGES

Ones admire Fours' creativity and connection to their inner world. Ones can use their connection to Fours to become more self-aware and emotionally honest. Fours appreciate Ones' self-discipline, which can motivate Fours to be more objective and willing to sacrifice a few personal needs for the benefit of the family. When stress picks up at home, these two are going to clash because of their contrasting styles. When Fours are stressed, they can become highly reactive, which can sometimes prompt Ones to also get emotional. More often than not, however, Ones repress the urge to shout back or retaliate. Over time, the anger will build and eventually past hurts and blame will spill out.

CONFLICT RESOLUTION

Ones come from a logical point of view; Fours are empathetic and come from an emotional point of view. It's important for them to understand and acknowledge the strengths and necessities of both of these approaches. Ones can try connecting to Fours' emotional side through meaningful discussions; Fours can practice not taking things personally in order to avoid working themselves up.

TYPE ONE & TYPE FIVE

STRENGTHS
- Careful with finances
- Respect personal boundaries
- Rational and objective

CHALLENGES
- Difficulty showing direct emotion
- Shut down when hurt or angry
- Critical and judgmental

LIVING IN HARMONY

Ones and Fives at home have a great deal of respect for each other. They value a home where they feel safe, independent, and relaxed. They both enjoy spending nights at home playing interesting and intellectually stimulating games, or having a lively discussion over dinner. They want to keep dramatics out of the home as much as possible, so they both strive to be emotionally calm—and they expect others in the home to do the same. Ones appreciate Fives' even-keeled and calm nature when stress arises; Fives find Ones' wise discernment helpful for creating an environment where they can both thrive. Both look forward to coming home to a tidy and organized environment, which helps them think clearly and enjoy each other's company. They will probably find a way to pique each other's humor and carefree nature with the help of their shared connection to Sevens, who might be a mutual friend.

CHALLENGES

For Ones and Fives, the shared similarities (which once brought them together) can sometimes be a source of aggravation and conflict. For example, these Types are both logical and pretty reserved. They respect these values in each other, but when it comes time to express emotions, it won't come easy to either of them, making it extremely difficult to strengthen their emotional bonds. If too much stress crops up between them at home, they will grow distant and resigned.

CONFLICT RESOLUTION

Healthy emotional bonds are important to maintain in a family. When conflict arises, it's important for these two Types to welcome each other's emotions. It doesn't have to be an intense crying session or a discussion full of profound emotions, just a conversation to let the other person know when they're feeling hurt or upset. They'll be able to understand each other on an emotional level without either feeling overwhelmed.

TYPE ONE & TYPE SIX

STRENGTHS
- Faithful and committed
- Rely on each other's support
- Guided by their shared beliefs

CHALLENGES
- Fret about the future
- Sensitive to criticism
- Want perfection

LIVING IN HARMONY

Ones and Sixes share similar beliefs, ideals, and parenting styles. Sixes bring warmth and commitment to a family dynamic; they are known for their fierce loyalty to those they love. Ones coexisting with Sixes can be very complementary; they both know how to sacrifice for the greater good and value their responsibilities within the family. They also both want to have fun and spend time together—but only if household chores and errands are done first. Ones appreciate Sixes for their perseverance through difficult times. When Ones are going through a stressful time, they know they can count on Sixes for support and compassion, which strengthens their bond over time. Sixes value Ones' need for doing the right thing and feel secure knowing Ones are consistent, discerning, and honorable. They both find happiness and comfort spending quality time together.

CHALLENGES

Both of these Types can be prone to procrastination. Sixes may put off making a family decision due to a lack of self-confidence; Ones may delay doing their homework or finishing a house project because of their need for everything to be done perfectly. Ones and Sixes both want to do things the right way, and will be hard on themselves if things don't work out that way. Both Types place heavy burdens of responsibility on themselves—burdens that stress them out and cause them to turn against each other. Ones will become angry with Sixes for projecting their negative thoughts onto them. Sixes become defensive and spiral downward when they feel things are not right between them.

CONFLICT RESOLUTION

Ones need to extend patience and reassurance to Sixes during conflict in order for them to feel safe, while Sixes should avoid becoming overly emotional and remain calm and direct. A solution would be to talk about the issues instead of making what could be very false assumptions. This plan builds trust and emotional safety for both of them.

TYPE ONE & TYPE SEVEN

STRENGTHS
- Value their personal space
- Complementary differences
- Highly supportive of each other

CHALLENGES
- Impatient and easily frustrated
- Arrogant and compulsive
- Can become hyperactive

LIVING IN HARMONY

These two Types are opposites and also share an arrow on the Enneagram. Sevens bring enthusiasm, positivity, and play to the family dynamic; Ones bring discipline, structure, and intentionality. Ones move toward Sevens when they're feeling secure and relaxed, which allows these two personalities to enjoy each other's company. They can bond over planning a family adventure or having a light-hearted conversation over dinner. These two, if self-aware, bring a balance of logic and optimism to a household. Ones really enjoy the way Sevens remind them to not take themselves so seriously. Sevens have a carefree energy about them that allows Ones to relax and enjoy the brighter side of life. Sevens admire how reliable Ones can be and usually feel very safe and grounded in their presence. Both of them enjoy learning and being inspired.

CHALLENGES

Sevens seek beauty and pleasure in life. They prefer their family members to stay optimistic and have fun. Ones have a slightly different approach to life: They want to have fun with the family as well, but not before the household duties are accomplished. As a result, Ones become easily frustrated with what they perceive as Sevens' self-indulgence and lack of discipline. Sevens will often find Ones' priorities limiting and unyielding.

CONFLICT RESOLUTION

The best way for these two Types to coexist is for them to strike a balance between their different approaches to life. Ones need to practice being less rigid with rules, guidelines, or expectations. This will help lighten the entire household. Sevens can learn from Ones' thrift and their ability to self-sacrifice every once in a while for the greater good of the family. Both benefit greatly by recognizing the strengths in each other.

TYPE ONE & TYPE EIGHT

STRENGTHS
- Protective and strong
- Passion for righting wrongs
- Able to sacrifice when needed

CHALLENGES
- Both want to be in charge
- Difficulty admitting fault
- Trouble with anger

LIVING IN HARMONY

At home, Ones and Eights are all about staying fair, doing the right thing, and being there for each other, no matter what. Both have a lot of energy and will work late nights or multiple jobs in order to make ends meet. In a family unit, Ones and Eights can foster a deep well of respect for each other. Ones admire the protectiveness and determination that Eights have for the family's well-being. Eights trust Ones' words and actions due to their strong moral compass. Both of them will want to bring safety, comfort, and stability to their home. When it comes to household priorities, these two Types have pretty strong convictions on rules, values, procedures, parenting styles, and responsibilities; when they agree, it will be very beneficial to the family. If not, it will be a power struggle between them.

CHALLENGES

Both of these Types live in the Body Center (also known as the Instinctual Center), which has an emotional pattern of anger. Ones usually repress their anger until it boils over, which can be very explosive. Eights' anger is readily available and often expressed. This typically becomes a problem when either of them wants to take control, or is not getting their needs met. Ones can be taken aback by Eights' aggressiveness; Eights can easily get angry at Ones if they sense any kind of hypocrisy. If either of these Types are children, they might exhibit some challenging behavior in order to maintain their independence and desire for autonomy.

CONFLICT RESOLUTION

If anything unfortunate is going to happen in this relationship, it'll be due to anger, arguments, or the need for control. Eights will provoke Ones to test their loyalty. Ones don't want to fight, but will have no issue engaging if confronted. They do have their limits, but once pushed, they will not back down. It's important for these Types to get control of their anger and practice healthy ways to release it on their own. It will be detrimental to the family if each other's anger issues are not addressed.

TYPE ONE & TYPE NINE

STRENGTHS
- Want a steady life
- Enjoy spending time outside
- Thrive with daily routines

CHALLENGES
- Stubborn
- Hold in their feelings
- Power struggles

LIVING IN HARMONY

Ones and Nines are both idealists who want to be at home in a peaceful and clean environment. They're both content with familiarity and will likely want to have regular routines so life at home feels predictable. Having family traditions will also be something important to the both of them. They will both be open to each other's views on how the family dynamics can be improved and will pride themselves on having a loving and stable home. Ones appreciate the calming and soothing nature Nines bring to a home. They find that they can be themselves because of Nines' nonjudgmental nature. This allows Ones to be less critical of themselves. Nines can often be indecisive or apathetic, making them grateful that Ones typically make most of the decisions.

CHALLENGES

Ones can be uptight about rules and cleanliness, whereas Nines are much more relaxed and can lean toward being messy. This will definitely be a recurring point of contention because Ones are typically bound and determined to keep a tidy home. Nines won't really understand why Ones get so worked up; their apathetic demeanor fuels Ones' anger. Both these Types also have a tendency to be passive-aggressive.

CONFLICT RESOLUTION

It's really important for these two to find compromise with each other in order to maximize harmony in the home. Ones need to be more patient and help Nines when they are having trouble making a decision and moving into action. Nines respond better to encouragement than criticism. Nines need to make sure they're speaking up for themselves. If they're not ready to answer or decide, they need to learn how to express that in a clear and constructive way.

TYPE TWO & TYPE TWO

STRENGTHS
- Enjoy quality time together
- Value emotional closeness
- Friendly and compassionate

CHALLENGES
- Emotionally manipulative
- Tendency to be intrusive
- Easily feel disconnected

LIVING IN HARMONY

Twos in the same household will have a mutual understanding about how the other views the world. Over time, they will bond because of their inclination toward emotional connection and their desire to want to be that special person in each other's lives. Twos can be nurturing, affectionate, and selfless, and are likely to develop a very close relationship.

CHALLENGES

Twos are highly sensitive, not only to criticism but also to the emotions of those they are close to. If one of them is feeling down, the other is likely to follow suit. Twos might feel upset if the other leaves them feeling left out, not needed, or unloved. Their arguments may lead to emotional outbursts or tears.

CONFLICT RESOLUTION

Twos should spend quality time together so they can get to know each other on an emotional level. They both appreciate the other taking interest in what brings them joy. Twos also appreciate words of affirmation, reassuring them that they are loved and needed. Twos often have a tendency to be overly focused on attending to the other's desires. They should remind each other to check in with themselves so they don't neglect their own needs.

TYPE TWO & TYPE THREE

STRENGTHS
- Thrive on each other's positive energy
- Encouraging and validating
- Friendly and polite

CHALLENGES
- Emotionally deceptive
- Needy for attention and praise
- Self-conscious

LIVING IN HARMONY

Twos and Threes want to live a happy life, surrounded by love and supportive people. They do well in any dynamic, but particularly in close quarters they're able to encourage, nurture, and praise each other often. They're both kind, personable, and can usually tell what the other needs. Over time, they are very likely to become the best of friends. Living together should prove to be a mutual benefit for both of them. Twos will feel loved and understood with Threes at home, and Threes will receive the recognition from Twos that they so deeply need.

CHALLENGES

Twos are ordinarily focused on their relationships. They are able to know what Threes need even before Threes are aware of it. Threes may not notice Twos' efforts as they are too concentrated on setting and accomplishing their goals. In those cases, Twos will become disheartened and feel unneeded. Threes might become annoyed that they have to stop what they are focused on in order to affirm Twos.

CONFLICT RESOLUTION

Twos can help Threes get in touch with their emotional side by making sure they feel safe and by letting them know they accept them for who they are, no matter what. Threes can help Twos set goals for themselves and encourage them to attend to their needs. They can support each other by reminding the other to look inward more. This allows Twos and Threes more opportunity to connect to their own feelings, wants, and desires.

TYPE TWO & TYPE FOUR

STRENGTHS
- Strong emotional connection
- Self-expressive
- Empathetic

CHALLENGES
- Overly dramatic
- Tend to get sad often
- Engage in a push-and-pull dynamic

LIVING IN HARMONY

Twos and Fours typically connect very easily over their love of beauty, creativity, and compassion for humankind. They are both afraid of expressing themselves, but they find comfort and safety in each other's presence. While they have no issue with darker emotions, they also relish making each other laugh. They have a strong sense of what the other is going through, and can help each other find the irony and humor in their more painful emotions.

CHALLENGES

Together, Twos and Fours have a lot of emotions to sort through. Fours can be temperamental and have a fear of being abandoned that can cause them to feel jealous or angry if Twos make other friends. They may feel as though they are being replaced and begin to withdraw. Twos could easily interpret this as a sign of rejection and become caught up in why Fours have become distant. Twos might be too prideful to tell Fours how they really feel; Fours might stay away, unable to get over their feelings of what they perceive as being scorned.

CONFLICT RESOLUTION

Since there will always be lots of feelings between these two, it will help their relationship if they both work out their emotions separately. Twos can practice tending to their own needs and not place expectations on Fours to behave in a certain way. Fours can remember to check in once in a while with Twos. Fours can help them in their time of need but also encourage them to explore their emotions on their own.

TYPE TWO & TYPE FIVE

STRENGTHS
- Understanding
- Gentle and kind
- Complementing strengths

CHALLENGES
- Sensitive and prideful
- Unable to ask for what they need
- Repress their wants

LIVING IN HARMONY

Twos and Fives have complementing strengths: Twos are in touch with their emotions and help Fives bring theirs to the surface. Fives may be reserved with their feelings at first, but slowly, at their own pace, they will feel safe enough to express how they feel with Twos. When Twos lean too heavily on their emotions, Fives can help them bring balance by displaying composure and steadiness. This pair may not immediately connect, but with time and patience, their relationship has the potential to grow into a tender friendship.

CHALLENGES

Twos will naturally need more time with Fives than Fives feel they're capable of giving. They might push too hard and cause Fives to retreat or become agitated by Twos' need for attention. Twos are likely to ruminate over experiences they have with Fives. They'll spend a great deal of time trying to figure out what they're thinking and feeling.

This can lead them to feeling exhausted from always questioning what their encounters mean.

CONFLICT RESOLUTION

Twos should understand that Fives do not need to be so emotionally invested with the friends they have. Yes, they enjoy their company and talking about common interests, but they aren't interested in diving deep into emotional conversations. Twos have to also respect Fives' need for space and privacy. Fives shouldn't shut out Twos when they feel overwhelmed by their presence. Instead, they can practice letting them know when they need a bit of space. Both of them will need to remind the other that even though they show it differently, they do in fact care for each other.

TYPE TWO & TYPE SIX

STRENGTHS
- Family-oriented
- Loyal, especially to family and friends
- Warm and friendly

CHALLENGES
- Insincere
- Fear of abandonment
- Can be easily taken advantage of

LIVING IN HARMONY

With a lot in common, Twos and Sixes can easily find a friend in the other. They're both warm and sensitive people who want to belong to a tightly knit group of friends. Twos get along great with Sixes because they're service-oriented like them, and they both enjoy helping others. Sixes want to become friends with Twos because their warm and nurturing personality allows Sixes to feel safe and calm. A friendship between Twos and Sixes usually develops easily thanks to their mutual respect and admiration for each other.

CHALLENGES

Twos and Sixes can easily become too dependent on each other, causing them both to lose autonomy and independence. They lack a bit of self-confidence and might rely too heavily on each other to be there as their "comfort blanket." This won't seem to be an issue at first, but over time, Sixes will feel smothered by Twos always coming to the rescue, and Twos will tire of having to always reassure Sixes that everything is going to be okay.

CONFLICT RESOLUTION

Twos and Sixes will need to help each other be more self-reliant, independent, and self-assured. To do this, they can allow the other to concentrate on themselves instead of placing the focus on each other. Twos have a natural inclination to neglect their needs. Sixes can support them by not running to them every time they have a problem. Twos can be there for their friend, but they'll need to make sure to establish a healthy boundary so that they do not become overly consumed by Sixes' problems.

TYPE TWO & TYPE SEVEN

STRENGTHS
- Positive thinkers
- Generous and kind
- Value a happy and fun atmosphere

CHALLENGES
- Deny negative emotions
- Difficulty receiving help
- Contrasting values

LIVING IN HARMONY

Twos and Sevens are both optimistic people who like to focus on the bright side of life. They enjoy being playful, outgoing, and sociable. Twos can sometimes be too timid to take risks, so Sevens offer them their spontaneous and adventurous spirit. Twos appreciate being taken out of their comfort zone and typically end up having a great time. Twos can remind Sevens how to appreciate emotional connectedness, which they can sometimes forget about.

CHALLENGES

Twos and Sevens have very different values. Twos seek out deep connections to their friends and people they care about. Sevens are more focused on their personal independence, freedom, and ways they can enjoy themselves. It's likely that Twos will sometimes feel as though Sevens are too busy with their own lives to spend time with them. Sevens, if not given their freedom or if made to feel guilty about the things they do, will begin to feel held back by Twos and may not want to be around them as much.

CONFLICT RESOLUTION

If Sevens need their own space, Twos will often move toward them in order to not lose them—even if Sevens aren't actually headed in that direction at all. Regardless, Sevens' distance will feel somewhat like abandonment or rejection to Twos, and they'll want to move toward them in an effort to "get them back." Sevens, on the other hand, move away from situations that are stressful and make them uneasy. Twos and Sevens need to stay still and be present in the moment. Instead of moving forward or away, they should communicate their negative emotions and clear the air. By doing this, they can understand where the other is coming from and adjust their behavior accordingly.

TYPE TWO & TYPE EIGHT

STRENGTHS
- Loyal and supportive
- Generous and protective
- Complementary strengths

CHALLENGES
- Overly dramatic
- Turbulent highs and lows
- Emotional outbursts

LIVING IN HARMONY

Twos and Eights can see a great deal of themselves in each other. Some of the strengths that Eights have, such as directness and strength, are something Twos find themselves needing in order to establish healthy boundaries for themselves. Eights enjoy living with Twos because it allows them to tap into their vulnerability since they feel safe to explore deeper topics with them. They usually admire in one another what they themselves are lacking.

CHALLENGES

Twos and Eights are on different energetic levels. Twos are upbeat and positive, and Eights tend to be more grounded and vigilant in their environment. This can create issues when Twos just want to hang out and have fun, but Eights are unable to relax their heightened senses and enjoy themselves. Twos might try to ease Eights' nerves, only to be met with hostility. Eights might feel as though they are being manipulated, so they'll refuse to back down out of the need to control the situation. As a result, Twos feel rejected or scared, and Eights feel frustrated that they have to walk on eggshells around Twos.

CONFLICT RESOLUTION

Twos and Eights should place more energy on themselves than on the other person. Twos should work on building their own assertive power instead of focusing on how Eights are feeling inside a situation. Eights can turn their fiery energy into understanding their emotions a bit better. This will help calm their impulses to be less reactive. Since they have complementing strengths, it's in the best interest of their relationship that they work on themselves to bring even more to each other in the end.

TYPE TWO & TYPE NINE

STRENGTHS
- Caring and kind
- Enjoy creating a happy atmosphere
- Accepting of others' differences

CHALLENGES
- Struggle with boundaries
- Allow people to walk over them
- Deny or avoid difficult feelings

LIVING IN HARMONY

When they meet, Twos and Nines feel instantly accepted by each other. They are generally relationship-oriented and enjoy being in each other's company. Twos and Nines speak the same language; they are helpful, nurturing, and accommodating. These two will rarely argue over much. They'd prefer to keep the peace. Twos enjoy Nines' undemanding nature and they feel as though they can truly be themselves around them. Nines like living with Twos because of their positive and often peppy energy.

CHALLENGES

Twos and Nines tend to quickly merge with the people they live with; they become like them or change themselves to accommodate the other person. Eventually, they may not know how they feel or what they truly want. Or, they'll come to a standstill because neither of them can make a decision. Twos may try to push Nines to take some course of action, which will make Nines feel pressured and stressed. They'll want to numb themselves from the uncomfortable emotions that continue to arise. Twos may become overly controlling and only push harder as Nines retreat.

CONFLICT RESOLUTION

Twos and Nines need to establish their own personal boundaries to prevent them from automatically merging with the other. In this way, they'll be able to enjoy each other's company without expectations or control. Bringing more awareness to how they feel and what they want as individuals will help both of them be more assertive in asking for what they want. Together, they can encourage each other to communicate their desires and opinions.

TYPE THREE & TYPE THREE

STRENGTHS

- Not overly sentimental
- Encouraging and motivating
- Enjoy being positive

CHALLENGES

- Overly high expectations
- Power struggles
- Difficulty letting go

LIVING IN HARMONY

Threes make some of the best friends. They cheer each other on when they need encouragement and help each other reach their goals. These two will enjoy sharing stories about their successes and will throw a congratulatory party when either of them reaches a personal goal. Threes also appreciate luxury and enjoy having a great time at a new bar or restaurant. They're usually the first to know about all the exciting events happening in town.

CHALLENGES

Neither of them wants to talk about their feelings. Threes tend to want to dodge those kinds of conversations. This will eventually turn into an issue when one of them has something disheartening happen to them. They're not likely to open up to each other, which can make them both feel isolated. Threes have the skillful habit of compartmentalizing their feelings. They think it's much more productive to set feelings aside and continue on without having true intimacy in their relationship.

CONFLICT RESOLUTION

If Threes want to form a strong bond with each other, they'll need to slow down their bodies and their minds, practice some self-acceptance, and begin to let the other in. This process will be uncomfortable at first and some effort will definitely need to come from an authentic place. They don't have to force it; they just need to stay present when they notice their feelings start to come to the surface. Instead of pushing them to the side or repressing them, they can open up to each other and share what's going on inside.

TYPE THREE & TYPE FOUR

STRENGTHS
- Enjoy creative pursuits
- Enjoy friendly competition
- Emotionally sensitive

CHALLENGES
- Don't understand each other
- Tendency to obsess
- Contrasting approach to emotions

LIVING IN HARMONY

Threes and Fours typically bond over pursuing creative interests and enjoying some of the finer things in life. Threes are able to keep going even during times of turbulent emotions. Fours make great living companions to Threes by being authentic and encouraging Threes to become emotionally honest with themselves. These two have a lot to teach each other and realize quickly that they can balance out each other quite nicely.

CHALLENGES

Threes and Fours will experience some tension from time to time. Since Threes are about progress and are typically action-oriented, they might find that Fours are too involved in their emotions to participate in activities. Threes will not fully understand why Fours need the time that they do to process their inner world. Fours may feel as though Threes are being insensitive. Fours have a tendency to feel that their emotional intelligence is superior to that of Threes, whereas Threes may feel their accomplishments are superior to those of Fours'.

CONFLICT RESOLUTION

In stressful situations, Threes usually want to keep moving and be productive. Fours, on the other hand, tend to withdraw when under stress. Instead of doing more, Threes should learn to find peace and calm in the present moment, even when sitting with difficult emotions. Instead of putting them aside, they need to process them, like Fours. Fours need to resist the urge to withdraw so far into their comfort zone that it's difficult for them to come out. They can take a hint from their Three friends and put some of that energy into doing.

TYPE THREE & TYPE FIVE

STRENGTHS
- Not overly emotional
- Self-reliant
- Enjoy learning new things

CHALLENGES
- Conflicting energy levels
- Trouble sharing their feelings
- Arrogant

LIVING IN HARMONY

Threes and Fives are usually very respectful of each other's space and privacy. Fives enjoy spending time alone, reading and exploring their interests. Threes give them the space they need to focus on their goals and work-related activities. Both of them, especially if they have common interests, enjoy having interesting conversations and will seek advice from each other on topics they know the other is competent in.

CHALLENGES

There are times when Fives come across as detached, moody, or too much "in their head," which Threes interpret as cold or rude behavior.

More often than not, Fives just need some alone time to process and recharge. Threes are usually full of energy and can sometimes push Fives too hard by asking them too many questions about their day or pressuring them to do something they're not ready to do. Fives will want to retreat from this situation and, as a result, Threes are likely to feel rejected.

CONFLICT RESOLUTION

Threes need to understand that when Fives take time for themselves, it's usually for them to recharge, which they can only do when they're alone and without any expectations placed on them. Threes should avoid making them feel guilty for this behavior and instead respect their boundaries. Fives can practice sharing a bit more about how they're feeling and what they need. Threes do well when information is relayed to them directly, so Fives can feel free to let Threes know when they need some time alone.

TYPE THREE & TYPE SIX

STRENGTHS

- Enjoy connecting with others
- Respectful and generous
- Work hard and persevere

CHALLENGES

- Easily defensive
- Fear disapproval from family and friends
- Take on too many responsibilities

LIVING IN HARMONY

Threes and Sixes are both pretty responsible and courteous people. They typically get along well, as they share several fundamental values, like dependability, teamwork, and an appreciation of community. They both want to have a strong support network. Threes gain a greater sense of their self-worth not only from those they are affiliated with but also from very caring, warm, and compassionate Sixes.

Threes are there to cheer on and encourage Sixes, which is just what they need to take risks or accept a challenge.

CHALLENGES

Sixes tend to worry a lot and become anxious, especially under stress. Threes will try their best to cheer them up or help them see the bright side of things. Over time, however, this strategy will become an issue for them because Threes become frustrated and tired of having to prop up Sixes. Threes can easily become impatient and emotionally detached during conflict, which will create a lot of negative energy between them. Sixes' anxiety and Threes' impatience can easily lead to lots of bickering and complaining.

CONFLICT RESOLUTION

It's very important for Threes to get in touch with their emotions. They tend to completely push them aside during conflict, which will make it difficult for Sixes to feel seen and understood, since they are usually bringing too many emotions to the conflict. If Threes allow themselves to feel a bit more vulnerable and Sixes practice managing how to regulate their reactivity, these two will be able to get beyond their differences.

TYPE THREE & TYPE SEVEN

STRENGTHS
- Positive
- Friendly and sociable
- Value freedom to pursue their interests

CHALLENGES
- Self-awareness
- Don't like to be slowed down
- Self-centeredness

LIVING IN HARMONY

Threes and Sevens get along great because they share many similarities. They're upbeat, optimistic, and friendly people who just want to live their lives to the fullest. Neither of them wants to be limited in any way; because they share this approach to life, they usually give each other the personal space to do so. Threes get along great with Sevens because they are able to share their enthusiasm with them. Sevens enjoy being in the company of Threes, who are their cheerleaders, supporting their many ideas.

CHALLENGES

Since both of them like to get their own way, Threes and Sevens can run into issues when making decisions about the home. This can be anything from choosing decor to assigning chores and responsibilities. Threes are most efficient at problem-solving. Sevens are also great problem-solvers, but they are not inclined to recognize that there is any problem to begin with. It will usually fall on Threes to speak up about any concerns or issues related to Sevens.

CONFLICT RESOLUTION

It won't be easy for Threes and Sevens to get through conflict as they both tend to avoid it altogether. However, they need to realize that it's in their best interest to address their concerns as they happen. In order to do this, they'll both need to slow down and come into the present to express themselves. Then, they can focus on accepting and processing their emotions.

TYPE THREE & TYPE EIGHT

STRENGTHS	CHALLENGES
• Strong personalities	• Overly competitive
• Enjoy a challenge	• Impulsive
• Supportive and resilient	• Difficulty asking for help

LIVING IN HARMONY

Threes and Eights have so much in common. They are both assertive and comfortable asking for what they need and want. They're usually the kind of people who take the lead on what needs to get done around the house. Threes help Eights put plans into action in the most efficient way. Eights give Threes the kind of support and generosity that Threes need.

CHALLENGES

Threes and Eights can both want to be in charge and make decisions. This can become a point of contention if one wants to make a household change that the other disagrees with. They are inclined to have standoffs in which Threes justify why their way is better, and Eights become domineering and maybe even belittle Threes in order to get their way and take back control. Eights have difficulty letting go of control, which in turn drives Threes crazy because they feel they are competent enough to make decisions as well.

CONFLICT RESOLUTION

It's important for Threes and Eights to work on building trust, which will ensure they have a mutual respect for the other's opinions, thoughts, concerns, or actions. It's vital that these two avoid the inclination to correct, micromanage, or persuade each other. They can both practice being more vulnerable, sharing more of their heart, and extending their own form of empathy and compassion for the other.

TYPE THREE & TYPE NINE

STRENGTHS
- Optimistic and sociable
- Easily adaptable
- Supportive of each other

CHALLENGES
- Dissociated from reality
- Conflict-avoidant
- Difficulty being emotionally honest

LIVING IN HARMONY

Threes and Nines coexist quite nicely together. They both prefer to live in a predictable environment with calm vibes and positive energy. They adapt easily to changes and can help each other share responsibilities. Threes tend to have quite a bit more energy than Nines, but Nines will often find that it ignites their own energy. At the same time, Nines are great at showing Threes how to slow down and relax after a hard day's work.

CHALLENGES

These Types have very different values when it comes to what makes them happy. Threes are looking for recognition and success, whereas Nines are content with a peaceful home and loving relationships. That's not to say that Nines don't have goals or Threes don't value healthy relationships, but these things are not what inherently lights them up. This can easily become an issue at home if one or the other is feeling rejected or dismissed.

CONFLICT RESOLUTION

It's in this duo's best interest to face their grievances with each other head-on. If Threes are feeling unappreciated, they need to bring it up. If Nines are thinking that Threes are coming across as disingenuous, they should avoid sweeping it under the rug and try to talk it out. Both of them have a tendency to want to just breeze through problems or avoid conflict. If they want to live together in the peaceful environment that they both long for, however, they'll have to practice healthy conflict resolution.

TYPE FOUR & TYPE FOUR

STRENGTHS
- Close companionship
- Deep understanding of each other's needs
- Enjoy a beautiful and eclectic style

CHALLENGES
- Shy and withdrawn
- Hypersensitive
- Stubborn and controlling

LIVING IN HARMONY

Fours feel safe, understood, and comfortable with each other. This deep rapport comes from their recognizing the strengths and challenges within each other. They both have empathy and compassion for the other's struggles and are inclined to honor and hold space for the other person. They're both going to value how the other is open and willing to listen to how their day went. Fours tend to want their space filled with beautiful and meaningful pieces of art and furniture. They'll enjoy and be fascinated by each other's eclectic style.

CHALLENGES

Fours are naturally inclined to be emotional, moody, and temperamental. If either of them is having an off day, they won't be able to conceal it (even if they try). They're both so intuitive that they'll know something is wrong. If they're under stress, the tension will intensify rather quickly and they might become reactive toward each other. They'll both need comfort and love, which may not be possible for the other to give them while they're also in crisis. This will create a chain reaction of both of them feeling abandoned, misunderstood, or unlovable.

CONFLICT RESOLUTION

Fours need to practice cultivating an emotional balance within themselves. They carry a lot of emotions that are best worked through by gently removing themselves from their emotional states, into a deeper understanding that will ground and steady them. To avoid future arguments, both of them can make it a daily practice to be aware and mindful of their turbulent emotions.

TYPE FOUR & TYPE FIVE

STRENGTHS
- Enjoy quiet time to themselves
- Appreciate ironic humor
- Love exploring interesting topics

CHALLENGES
- Spend too much time in their heads
- Struggle with connecting to their bodies
- Overly private and secretive

LIVING IN HARMONY

Fours and Fives can make quite an unconventional couple. They don't like the ordinary and prefer their decor be unique and well made. Their home might be decorated in a very particular manner that allows for both of them to express who they are. They're respectful of each other's tastes and preferences, which is beneficial when sharing a space. Both of them are open-minded and thoroughly enjoy talking about common interests. Although they delight in each other's company, they also respect each other's space and privacy.

CHALLENGES

Fours are deeply emotional and typically let their feelings guide their decisions, whereas Fives are more detached from their emotions and guided by their thoughts. Fives are much more rational and will probably take the lead to make sure the household runs smoothly. At times, they might be bothered by how emotional Fours can be. Fours will often feel sad that they can't connect more with Fives.

CONFLICT RESOLUTION

Fours and Fives have very different ways of dealing with their emotions and responding to stress. Fours should practice steadying their feelings and being mindful about their reactivity, especially when trying to resolve conflicts with the other. This will help prevent Fives from withdrawing and encourage them to remain present during conflict resolution. They can both practice how to effectively deal with stress.

TYPE FOUR & TYPE SIX

STRENGTHS
- Reassuring and friendly
- Empathetic and kind
- Understand each other's emotional tendencies

CHALLENGES
- Highly reactive
- Tendency to play devil's advocate
- Several insecurities

LIVING IN HARMONY

Fours and Sixes thrive in a warm and supportive environment. They both feel safe coming home and expect to be received with love and connection. They do well in this kind of environment as it supports their need to feel as though they belong. Fours and Sixes can be vulnerable with each other, knowing that they will always be treated with love and acceptance. Sixes don't want to lose the support of Fours, so they'll typically become compliant to what they need. Fours will make sure to be there to reassure Sixes and help build their self-confidence.

CHALLENGES

When under stress, Fours can become aloof and possibly arrogant and dismissive. This reaction may be their way of covering their own insecurities. Unable to understand how to interpret Fours' behavior, Sixes may become anxious and start to question Fours' loyalty to them. And, because Sixes are so highly reactive, any disagreements they have with Fours can easily become emotionally volatile.

CONFLICT RESOLUTION

Fours and Sixes are very emotional during conflict. It is in their best interest to first steady their emotions on their own before approaching each other. They both need to understand that they both have a fear of abandonment, so they need to practice being aware of how their own behaviors and words might be affecting the other. It can strengthen their relationship for both of them to strengthen their inner sense of security.

TYPE FOUR & TYPE SEVEN

STRENGTHS
- Idealistic and passionate
- Prefer to go against the grain
- Enjoy feeling special and unique

CHALLENGES
- Tendency to be snobby
- Self-indulgent
- Impatient and demanding

LIVING IN HARMONY

Although Fours and Sevens are quite different from each other, those differences create a nice balance at home. Fours are emotional and creative; Sevens are optimistic and enjoy having new experiences. Sevens are able to take Fours out of their comfort zone and encourage them to have more fun and be more spontaneous. Fours are able to slow down Sevens and create a space for them where they feel safe to talk about their emotions. Living together, Fours and Sevens recognize how the strengths within each other can balance out their challenges.

CHALLENGES

Fours tend to be a lot more introverted than Sevens, which will create problems when it comes to socializing. Fours enjoy their time alone and their privacy, and don't appreciate unexpected visitors. Sevens, on the other hand, love having people over, enjoy hosting, and want to have fun experiences that they can share with family and friends. Fours might get hostile toward Sevens if they feel that their boundaries are not being respected. Sevens will get frustrated that they are not able to enjoy themselves in their own home.

CONFLICT RESOLUTION

Fours and Sevens are so different that they need to practice accepting and tolerating each other's opinions, thoughts, ideas, and preferences. They can do this by learning about the other's needs. It will be essential for these two to come together and work out the boundaries they both need in order to feel safe and content at home. It is somewhat easier for them to navigate their differences and resolve conflicts because Sevens want to avoid conflict and maintain a peaceful and happy environment.

TYPE FOUR & TYPE EIGHT

STRENGTHS
- Passionate and intense
- Enjoy excitement and feeling alive
- Authentic

CHALLENGES
- Impulsive and reckless
- Emotionally volatile
- Tendency to dominate

LIVING IN HARMONY

Fours and Eights foster a tremendous amount of warmth, empathy, and safety at home. Fours appreciate how generous and big-hearted Eights can be, which also feeds their need for acceptance and belonging. When it comes to getting things done, Eights appreciate how intense and purposeful Fours can become. Over time, they are likely to develop a significant amount of respect for each other's space, autonomy, and energies.

CHALLENGES

Fours and Eights do not want to be controlled in any way. In their attempt to be understood, Fours can become emotionally domineering, which Eights may easily interpret as manipulative and controlling. Eights, who are inclined to move rather quickly into confrontation, will not stand for this and will not back down. Arguments between these two will turn into a battle of who's in control and who has the power. When tensions rise, both of them can provoke the other into creating a highly volatile situation.

CONFLICT RESOLUTION

In order to live in a harmonious environment, Fours and Eights need to learn how to regulate their emotions, temper their reactivity, and tame their impulses. These two would benefit from sitting down with each other to check in with how the other is doing. They should come together in a safe, neutral headspace, where they are able to voice their concerns in an unemotional and rational manner. If they diligently practice this, it will cut down on their arguments and strengthen their bonds.

TYPE FOUR & TYPE NINE

STRENGTHS
- Understanding and accepting
- Sensitive to other's needs
- Relationship-oriented

CHALLENGES
- Feelings of inferiority
- Self-deprecating
- Tendency to withdraw

LIVING IN HARMONY

Fours and Nines have several similarities: Both are quite spiritual, creative, and highly intuitive, and they enjoy a peaceful and quiet home environment where they are able to express who they are and be themselves without fear of criticism. Nines are already accepting of others, which allows Fours to feel safe and rarely misunderstood. Nines are inclined to repress how they feel and what they want; Fours, however, will quickly pick up on this and help them freely voice their needs and desires.

CHALLENGES

Fours have a tendency to be dramatic and may experience several mood swings a day. This will cause Nines to withdraw—they do not want to ride Fours' emotional roller coaster. Nines repress their anger, but it will eventually come out in a passive-aggressive way; Fours will not understand how to interpret this unexpected anger. Instead, they will begin to dislike how withdrawn and stubborn Nines have become. Both of them will eventually withdraw from the other.

CONFLICT RESOLUTION

Fours and Nines actually have the advantage of wanting to return to each other. Neither wants conflict and both want to stop whatever internal pain they are experiencing. They will need to learn to deal with conflict in a more effective manner. Fours should practice using coping mechanisms to managing their stress, such as asking to take a break from the conflict and going out for a walk. Nines can draw on their own coping mechanisms for handling stress, such as staying present and offering ideas to solve the conflict.

TYPE FIVE & TYPE FIVE

STRENGTHS
- Honest and understanding
- Respect each other's privacy
- Enjoy stimulating conversations

CHALLENGES
- Overly analytical
- Emotionally unavailable
- Cynical and sarcastic

LIVING IN HARMONY

Two Fives living together are going to understand the nuances of their preferences, such as their need for emotional space, time alone, and privacy. Fives appreciate a quiet and tranquil environment. They are typically organized and prefer the sense of order that comes from having daily routines. Fives come together to have stimulating conversations, discuss exciting ideas, and share their thoughts. They might even enjoy the occasional friendly debate.

CHALLENGES

Fives are inherently emotionally detached; that does not mean that they don't have or show feelings, however. Sometimes, one of them will want more attention or need to spend time with the other. When one of them does not have the energy to be social, this can cause the other to feel ignored or rejected—and wanting to withdraw. Because neither of them will want to approach the other about how they are feeling, they will feel distant from each other and maybe even emotionally empty.

CONFLICT RESOLUTION

A mutual understanding of each other's needs is essential for Fives to coexist peacefully. For example, if one of them requires spending a few hours alone after they get home from work or school to decompress and regain their energies, the other will need to respect this and allow them their space. The best way to learn about each other is to open up and have friendly discussions about what their boundaries are so that expectations are out in the open.

TYPE FIVE & TYPE SIX

STRENGTHS
- Loyal and kind
- Levelheaded in a crisis
- Curious

CHALLENGES
- Hypervigilant
- Pessimistic and cynical
- Spend too much time in their heads

LIVING IN HARMONY

Fives and Sixes intellectually spark each other. They both enjoy contemplating and reflecting on their experiences. They are likely to have quite a collection of books in their home that reveals their personal interests. When Sixes feel comfortable and safe, they allow Fives to have as much space and freedom as they need. Both of them value living in a steady and predictable environment. Fives also appreciate the warmth and friendliness that Sixes offer.

CHALLENGES

Issues arise at home when Sixes are feeling anxious or fearful. Fives will not be able to give them the reassurance and comfort that they need and will begin to withdraw if they think Sixes need too much of them. This only perpetuates Sixes' skepticism about whether or not they can trust or depend on Fives. Fives will often find it exhausting contending with Sixes' irrational thinking.

CONFLICT RESOLUTION

It's important for Fives and Sixes to recognize that they both deal with a lot of anxiety in different ways. When Fives are feeling anxious, they tend to withdraw into themselves; when Sixes feel anxious, they reach out to others for reassurance. This means that Fives will have to tend to matters of the heart for Sixes, and Sixes will need to learn how to self-soothe if Fives are unavailable. Both of them can benefit from practicing ways of calming the mind.

TYPE FIVE & TYPE SEVEN

STRENGTHS
- Great storytellers
- Enjoy experimenting with new ideas
- Complement each other's challenges

CHALLENGES
- Self-involved
- Pushing their ideas onto others
- Anxious and restless

LIVING IN HARMONY
Fives and Sevens get along well together at home. They are both independent people who enjoy their freedom and autonomy. They have no issues respecting each other's space and both enjoy learning from each other. Fives and Sevens are in the Thinking Triad, which means they will have a mutual mental connection. Fives typically think their energy is limited but living with Sevens allows them to tap into their energy, which they very much appreciate. Sevens love how intelligent Fives are and will often seek them out for advice.

CHALLENGES
Fives prefer a more tranquil and quiet environment. The energy that Sevens exude is usually very stimulating and can be overwhelming to Fives at times. They won't want to cause any conflict, but they will probably leave the room until they feel it's safe for them to return. If Sevens have friends over, Fives might just stay in their room to avoid the crowd. Sevens won't be easily offended by this, but they might start thinking that Fives are boring, no fun, or even snobby.

CONFLICT RESOLUTION

These two can live in harmony if they allow the other to express their needs and if they're both willing to compromise a little. Fives will need to open up about what makes them feel uncomfortable. Sevens should avoid making Fives feel odd for having certain needs; it will only make them feel insecure. Sevens will have to be more aware of how their high energy might be affecting Fives. If they notice Fives becoming overwhelmed, they can simply bring their energy level down a few notches.

TYPE FIVE & TYPE EIGHT

STRENGTHS
- Observant and trustworthy
- Value their personal space
- Self-reliant

CHALLENGES
- Arrogant and dismissive
- Overly correcting each other
- Battle for control

LIVING IN HARMONY

Fives and Eights balance out each other. Since they're both independent and don't want to be controlled, they don't rely on each other very much for emotional connection or favors. They're both highly self-sufficient. Fives deal with anxiety from time to time; Eights' energy calms Fives and allows them to relax knowing that Eights' protective "I have this under control" force is present. When Eights react too quickly, Fives can use their insight and objectivity to slow down Eights' impulses.

CHALLENGES

Fives and Eights have different ways of coping with tension at home: Fives either withdraw or become anxious and irritable; Eights become controlling and aggressive. These styles don't necessarily complement each other, so this is an area where these two will come in conflict. If there is an issue, Eights will hash it out with Fives without hesitation.

Fives, however, will find this approach abrasive and will likely shut down and stonewall Eights.

CONFLICT RESOLUTION

Fives will need to develop thicker skin and a healthy way to stand their ground with Eights. When Fives are able to resist withdrawing, Eights gain respect for them and are less likely to become aggressive because they are no longer being triggered. Eights will need to practice harnessing their energy and becoming more aware of how it aggravates Fives' sense of unease. If these two develop a respect for each other's differences, they can find solutions to their problems much faster.

TYPE FIVE & TYPE NINE

STRENGTHS
- Gentle and kind
- Dependable and thoughtful
- Value their personal space

CHALLENGES
- Trouble expressing how they feel
- Emotional confusion
- Tendency to get lost in thought

LIVING IN HARMONY

Fives and Nines usually have a very supportive and calm relationship at home. They both want to live in an undisturbed environment where they are able to have plenty of time and space to themselves. Although they both allow the other to have the personal space they need, they are also content knowing the other is there. Neither of them pressures the other to engage. As they both dislike intrusiveness, this works out nicely. Fives feel safe and accepted by Nines, and Nines enjoy having deep and meaningful conversations with Fives.

CHALLENGES

When either of them has an unpleasant experience with the other, they'll tend to keep it to themselves because they prefer to avoid conflict. This can be anything from not cleaning up after themselves to having a conversation that left one of them feeling hurt. Neither of them will want to push the matter. Over time, these small grievances will build up and they'll both be holding onto them internally. It will eventually come out and will probably be passed on to the other passive-aggressively, until one of them finally confronts the other.

CONFLICT RESOLUTION

The issue here is that neither Fives nor Nines are very connected to their emotions and how they feel about certain things. Their emotions get buried and neither has the energy to address them. Fives need to practice connecting to the heart and Nines need to practice connecting to their anger. In order to live in harmony with each other, they will both have to accept that they'll need to have conflict resolution skills in order to truly overcome their issues. They can do this by encouraging each other to talk regularly, a little bit at a time. Instead of a two-hour conversation, they are better off having a thirty-minute chat once a week.

TYPE SIX & TYPE SIX

STRENGTHS	CHALLENGES
• Value trust and reliability	• Self-defeating
• Faithful to loved ones	• Struggle with self-doubt
• Playful and humorous	• Anxious and worrisome

LIVING IN HARMONY

Sixes are the people you can count on in a crisis. They're extremely loyal, steadfast, and can persevere through many trials. At home, they're usually the ones fully prepared for just about anything, from natural disasters to a Sunday picnic in the park. They have incredible foresight and are able to anticipate what may occur. They are also reassuring, caring, and are dedicated to those they live with. They want to make sure everyone feels included and safe.

CHALLENGES

Issues arise for Sixes when they both become worried and anxious about the same things. They can create cycles of doubt, brainstorming all possible outcomes; doing this over and over again usually pushes them into a state of panic. They might start to project these fears onto their loved ones and those they live with. They can become highly reactive and won't appreciate it if anyone tries to tell them to "calm down." In the moment, they think that whatever they are feeling is very real and don't want to be told otherwise. When they're both in this state, they're likely to be emotional and accusatory, and arguments will surely commence.

CONFLICT RESOLUTION

Both of them need to work on their own anxieties and learn methods of self-soothing. They need to understand that they can't depend on the other to be their ultimate source of comfort; this only creates codependency. Instead, they can cooperate to find out what works for the other person, because it will likely be different. Even though they are the same Type, they will have different personal preferences regarding what behaviors allow them to feel safe and loved. They should also talk about things that put them into a state of doubt, fear, or panic, so that they can be mindful not to become each other's source of anxiety.

TYPE SIX & TYPE SEVEN

STRENGTHS
- Friendly and sociable
- Drawn to excitement
- Powerful foresight

CHALLENGES
- Difficulty soothing themselves
- Restless energy
- Overreactive

LIVING IN HARMONY

Sixes and Sevens are both very sociable. They like having family and friends over the house, enjoy going on outings with their loved ones, and delight in having stimulating conversations over dinner. Sixes usually shy away from trying new experiences but living with Sevens helps to draw out their adventurous spirit. Sevens are visionaries, but when it comes to planning, they typically only see the big picture. So, it's nice for them to have Sixes near to help them plan, manage, and pay attention to the details that Sevens may have overlooked.

CHALLENGES

These two approach the world quite differently. Sixes tend to be cautious, worrisome, and looking for threats, whereas Sevens are typically more optimistic, carefree, and impulsive. This is where they will run into issues. Sevens tend to be more self-involved—for example, they can forget to run errands or pick up dinner. Sixes may get frustrated with Sevens' lack of focus. Sevens can feel burdened by responsibilities. They'll both become anxious when their needs are not being met.

CONFLICT RESOLUTION

Both Sixes and Sevens let their anxiety get the best of them. This anxiety will be what perpetuates their arguments if they don't learn to manage it in a healthy way. They both need to slow down and spend some time with their thoughts, which will allow them to notice where their anxiety is coming from. After that, they can open up to each other. Sixes will have to strengthen their self-reliance. Sevens will need to practice mindfulness and resist the urge to use stimulation to avoid feeling anxious.

TYPE SIX & TYPE EIGHT

STRENGTHS
- Courageous
- Value their safety
- Trustworthy and dependable

CHALLENGES
- Hypervigilant
- Combative toward each other
- Inherently on the defensive

LIVING IN HARMONY

Sixes and Eights approach the world in similar ways. They are typically both on the defensive and alert to any outside threats. Sixes usually feel very safe living with Eights because Eights' strong self-confidence allows Sixes to let down their guard. Eights like that they can depend on Sixes to be there through tough times. Both of them are hardworking, responsible, and typically show their love through acts of service.

CHALLENGES

Sixes and Eights can both be quite aggressive and reactionary when they are in conflict. Sixes can easily unnerve Eights with their indecisive behavior and constant testing of their faithfulness. Either Sixes will feel unsafe and shy away from confrontation with Eights, or they will lash out and become just as aggressive. Most of their issues will manifest from their fears.

CONFLICT RESOLUTION

Both Sixes and Eights are afraid of being hurt, so their trust in each other will be tested from time to time. They'll both have to learn how to not project their fears onto each other. Sixes will need to practice how to stop worrying so much about the future, which will require them to stay in the present. Eights need to learn how to become more vulnerable and not allow their fears to manifest as anger.

TYPE SIX & TYPE NINE

STRENGTHS
- Empathetic
- Generous and supportive
- Value their relationships

CHALLENGES
- Overly accommodating
- Tendency to become codependent
- Seek safety from others

LIVING IN HARMONY

Sixes and Nines are generally loyal and caring toward each other. They both value kindness and consideration. They both want to make sure they clean up after themselves and honor their household commitments. Sixes tend to get nervous easily, and appreciate how patient and thoughtful Nines can be with their feelings. Sixes keep things steady and safe, which lines up perfectly with Nines' need for consistency.

CHALLENGES

Sixes easily become annoyed at Nines' aloofness. Nines have a tendency to be forgetful and unable to prioritize their responsibilities. This will drive Sixes crazy and make them feel as if they have to get after Nines to stay on the right track. This frustrates Nines and may even be enough to shut them down. Nines hate being pressured and will only become more stubborn in a passive-aggressive attempt to stand their ground.

CONFLICT RESOLUTION

These two can use self-soothing techniques to remain in the present in order to effectively handle conflict. Sixes need to make sure that they are not projecting their internal fears and insecurities onto

Nines. It is essential for Nines to remain present in the moment, even when they feel uncomfortable and unable to endure conflict. Nines need to persevere with Sixes. Both of them can encourage the other to voice their needs.

TYPE SEVEN & TYPE SEVEN

STRENGTHS
- Upbeat and spontaneous
- Highly resilient
- Value their independence

CHALLENGES
- Tend to run from their problems
- Struggle with staying present
- Overly self-involved

LIVING IN HARMONY

Sevens bring a lot of energy and liveliness to a home. They are optimists at heart and thrive in a positive and supportive environment. Together, Sevens will find it easy to find fun things to do. They won't ever have to worry about the other not being able to keep up, as they both have a great deal of energy. They enjoy swapping stories and bantering with each other. Sevens are also highly independent and prefer not to be tied to a schedule or a set of house rules.

CHALLENGES

Sevens can be incredibly scattered, impulsive, and undisciplined. They both have a tendency to neglect their needs, responsibilities, and possibly even their relationship with each other. When one of them tries to prohibit the other from doing what they want, it can upset Sevens and bring out their pushy, impulsive nature. When they make an attempt to rationalize their behavior to each other, they could end up throwing barbs or insensitive remarks at each other.

CONFLICT RESOLUTION

By nature, Sevens can be restless and easily bored, a result of them not being able to calm their anxieties. Instead, they resort to keeping busy, taking on too many projects, and maybe even engaging in manic behavior. They need to learn how to navigate through uncomfortable emotions in a healthy way. They need to both accept this about themselves and have compassion for the other when these behavioral patterns occur. They can help each other stay in the present and work through their difficulties together.

TYPE SEVEN & TYPE EIGHT

STRENGTHS

- Action-oriented
- Strive to live life to the fullest
- Self-assertive and generous

CHALLENGES

- Push themselves too hard
- Fixated on instant gratification
- Insensitive and self-serving

LIVING IN HARMONY

Sevens and Eights are both go-getters; at home, they put their energy into household activities or go out to run errands. They might enjoy hosting friends and loved ones, and tend to be the ones to lead group adventures. Both of them want to get all that they can out of life. Sevens enjoy Eights' bountiful energy, and Eights love the feeling of being alive—living with Sevens can be quite exhilarating for them.

CHALLENGES

When Sevens are not constantly in motion and keeping their minds busy, they can become restless with anxiety. They have a tendency to ignore their responsibilities, which infuriates Eights. Eights are responsible and reliable people who need to know that Sevens can be trusted. If Sevens don't come through, things could get ugly between these two. Sevens will not care for how Eights approach them, and

Eights may even begin to nag Sevens, which only makes matters worse.

CONFLICT RESOLUTION

Sevens and Eights are both disconnected from their heart in some way. The extent of the disconnection will determine how well these two will be able to build a genuine bond. They both need to get in touch with their emotions and open up to each other. Sharing this kind of intimacy with people they live with is essential to living in a compassionate home. Sevens should practice fully processing their negative emotions, and Eights should avoid using strength as a way to protect themselves. Their home needs to be a place of peace and safety for both of them.

TYPE SEVEN & TYPE NINE

STRENGTHS
- Positive mindset
- Very forgiving
- Can let things go easily

CHALLENGES
- Extremely conflict-avoidant
- Tendency to neglect responsibilities
- Out of touch with their emotions

LIVING IN HARMONY

Sevens and Nines get along really well. They both prefer to stay on the sunny side of life and value a happy and positive home environment. Instead of sweating the small stuff, both of them prefer to just let things go. Should anything unpleasant occur, they're willing to give the other person the benefit of the doubt. They're both quite open-minded and enjoy listening to each other's perspectives. Sevens appreciate that Nines don't put any pressure on them, which allows them to keep their independence and sense of autonomy. Nines enjoy coming alive with the exuberant energy that Sevens bring.

CHALLENGES

Sevens have a much stronger personality than Nines. They can become quite self-involved, so they can tend to worry about only themselves and overlook Nines' needs. Nines are conflict-averse; they do not want to bring up their grievances to Sevens. Nines will instead repress their anger, only to have it show up later in passive-aggressive behavior toward Sevens. Sevens don't want to have anything to do with Nines' attitude and most likely will just leave the situation altogether.

CONFLICT RESOLUTION

Both Sevens and Nines need to find a way to get in touch with their emotions and the unpleasant feelings that may arise between them at home. Instead of avoiding each other and ignoring their own internal conflicts, they should both find healthier ways to cope with conflict. When they cultivate a more positive approach to resolving their differences, it will benefit them not only as a unit but also individually. Only by remaining present with each other through the conflict will they be able to truly attend to unresolved hurt and anger.

TYPE EIGHT & TYPE EIGHT

STRENGTHS
- Generous and kind
- Value truth and honesty
- Strong-willed

CHALLENGES
- Overbearing
- Egocentric
- Quick to anger

LIVING IN HARMONY

Eights bring not only an abundance of energy into their home, but also an incredible amount of protectiveness, loyalty, and passion. Eights are action-oriented and focused on maintaining a safe and resilient household. They participate in plenty of friendly debates and discussions, and are likely to get involved in social activities in their community.

CHALLENGES

These two have so much energy between them that it will be difficult for them to slow down and relax. They are prone to work themselves past their limits, and will forget about how the other might be feeling or how their own behavior is affecting the other. Eights can be extremely unaware of how their actions and energy makes others feel. They might even seem as if they don't care, but it's more likely that they are moving so fast that they become aloof and eventually dismissive of each other's reactions.

CONFLICT RESOLUTION

At home, Eights may be so blinded by their need to control everything that happens there that they become hypervigilant, wanting to micromanage every move that the other makes. They both need to reach into their hearts and recognize that this need for power and control is a coping strategy, a way to compensate for the fear they have of being hurt or controlled. To find their way out of this challenging situation, Eights should work on managing their anger, impulses, and reactivity to conflict.

TYPE EIGHT & TYPE NINE

STRENGTHS	CHALLENGES
• Practical	• Stubborn
• Down-to-earth	• Can be unemotional
• Cherish comfort	• Controlling

LIVING IN HARMONY

Eights and Nines strive to cultivate a cozy and quiet environment at home. They both do well with routine and predictability, which allows them to feel safe, secure, and happy. They enjoy occasionally going out with loved ones, but usually prefer spending nights in together. Eights feel calm and steady with Nines around. Nines appreciate that Eights typically take the lead, allowing them to just go with the flow, which is what they prefer.

CHALLENGES

Eights and Nines have different energies and divergent approaches to conflict. Eights have no problem confronting Nines on any and every grievance they have. In contrast, Nines want to avoid conflict at all costs. When there is an issue that comes up between them, depending on the severity, these two may enter into a tense standoff. Eights will want to clear the air with a hearty argument, which only causes Nines to withdraw, fueling Eights' anger. Over time, this cycle of argument, withdrawal, and anger will repeat, leading to further resentment and rage.

CONFLICT RESOLUTION

Eights need to understand that confronting Nines is not the way to resolve their conflicts. They should find a calmer and more compassionate route to truly end disputes. Eights should work on controlling their temper as well as learning how to tap into their emotions (besides anger) to be able to have a heartfelt conversation with Nines. Nines, on the other hand, need to tap into their anger and learn how to express it, but they won't be able to unless they feel safe around Eights. Both of them must learn to compromise with each other over time; creating a safe place for them both is a key component of that understanding.

TYPE NINE & TYPE NINE

STRENGTHS
- Get along well
- Thoughtful and kind
- Accepting and compassionate

CHALLENGES
- Passive-aggressive
- Overly attached to their habits
- Difficulty prioritizing what's most important

LIVING IN HARMONY

Nines are all about trying to maintain a peaceful home environment. They both want to keep the house tidy and maybe even add creative touches here and there. They are thoughtful of the other's preferences and will likely go along with whomever displays the most energy when they make decisions. Nines enjoy each other's company, but they are also aware that the other needs their personal space. These two will probably live in a harmonious and functional home.

CHALLENGES

Nines' most challenging issue is that they both hold onto resentment. Although neither wants to admit or confront this fact, when they live together, it's impossible to avoid. Eventually, the unresolved issues that they've both avoided and buried within themselves emerge during a conflict (usually in a passive-aggressive way), causing them both to want to avoid the other. Both are prone to getting very sad about these hanging issues and can easily slip into numbing their pain in unhealthy ways.

CONFLICT RESOLUTION

Nines need to practice staying present in the conflict when it arises. This will help them release their anger, hurt, or other negative emotions. They'll benefit from checking in with each other daily and asking if there is anything that they'd like to get off their chest. They both need to be patient while waiting for the other to respond, but they should also encourage each other in a positive way to share their heart. They can let the other know that no matter what challenges get in the way of their relationship, they can work it out.

5

Using the Enneagram to Improve Romantic Relationships

TYPE ONE & TYPE ONE

STRENGTHS
- Value promises
- Witty and dry sense of humor
- Not overly sentimental

CHALLENGES
- Find it difficult to indulge
- Always want to be right
- Lets resentment build

LOVING IN HARMONY

Ones are drawn together in a relationship through their mutual respect for honesty and morals, and high standards for themselves and the people in their lives. Ones find comfort and solace knowing there is someone out there who also has their same coping mechanisms and core values. They are attracted to each other's wholesomeness and share a passion for righting the wrongs of the world. Ones have incredible self-restraint; they place duty above pleasure and admire that in each other. They can be deeply committed and have a great deal of trust in one another. This couple looks to each other for inspiration and support in their quest to become better people. They're both comfortable addressing their concerns and feel relieved that the other doesn't need anything "sugar-coated." They are straightforward and appreciate each other's direct speaking style.

CHALLENGES

Ones are hardworking individuals who take on extra work out of a sense of responsibility and pressure themselves to make sure it's done to their high standards. Together, they need to prioritize relaxation, fun, and quality time to foster pleasure and intimacy. When they burn themselves out, they operate from a place of frustration and will be quick to get angry.

CONFLICT RESOLUTION

It's imperative for this couple to learn how to communicate their needs to one another and talk through their emotions. Both of them will battle with their inner critic and will need the other to be compassionate, kind, and forgiving. Giving each other the benefit of the doubt will ease tension and allow for grace. Instead of correcting each other, they need to give each other encouragement and positive affirmation.

TYPE ONE & TYPE TWO

STRENGTHS
- Want to be of service to each other
- Enjoy being needed
- Want to make the world a better place

CHALLENGES
- High expectations
- Suppressed emotions
- Their anger can be explosive

LOVING IN HARMONY

There is a wonderful balance of warmth, logic, and companionship when Ones and Twos come together in love. Ones bring honor and realism to the relationship; Twos contribute empathy and affection. This pair shares an appreciation for generosity, responsibility, commitment, and trust. They also have a deep respect for each other's core values, making it very easy for them to fall in love and share excitement for their future. Ones are usually attracted to Twos' charm and generosity, and Twos love Ones' honest and forthright character. Ones feel valued; Twos feel safe. Another similarity in this pairing is how they view the world. They are both aware of its suffering and have a soft spot in their hearts for social causes. This couple is likely going to want to give back to others by volunteering or making sure they're available to help friends and family.

CHALLENGES

A common issue for this couple is Ones' lack of emotional connection. Ones can be very warm but Twos need a great deal of emotional connection and intimacy, which does not come naturally for

Ones. Ones, on the other hand, view Twos as too needy; because Ones value their autonomy, they will retreat from Twos, leaving Twos feeling abandoned.

CONFLICT RESOLUTION

Ones treasure their autonomy, which is why it's important that Twos develop their own independence. Ones will need to work on opening up and being emotionally available. Twos enjoy talking about their emotional experience and should gently encourage Ones to express themselves. When Ones need space or do not have the capacity to engage, they can avoid shutting out Twos by letting them know they just want some independence. Twos need to understand that they are not being rejected; they can learn how to show compassion by allowing Ones to take the space they need.

TYPE ONE & TYPE THREE

STRENGTHS
- Strong-willed and determined
- Always wanting to self-improve
- Objective and logical

CHALLENGES
- Self-critical
- Intimacy issues
- Overly focused on self-image

LOVING IN HARMONY

Together, Ones and Threes are classic overachievers who hold themselves to pretty high standards. They are a goal-oriented duo who share a desire to be competent, accomplished, and acknowledged for their efforts. They both have high energy, love to win, and value efficiency. These Types want to make each other proud and typically succeed at doing so. Ones are attracted to Threes' charm and social graces as well as their work ethic and drive to be the best at what they do. Threes love how Ones are incredibly focused, logical, and appreciative of quality over quantity. These two are probably going to be very focused on their careers and will relate to each other mostly on this level. They are not very connected to their emotions or interested in sharing intimate details, but, over time, they can definitely create emotional bonds. They tend to enjoy each other's company through task-oriented activities.

CHALLENGES

This couple may encounter problems because they're both hard on themselves, and they struggle to connect with each other on deeper emotional levels. Threes adapt quickly and are able to become whatever the public wants them to be; this is a major turnoff for Ones, who value honesty and integrity. Threes thrive on positive attention, and resent the judgment and criticism Ones bring to the relationship.

CONFLICT RESOLUTION

Ones can resist viewing things as black and white, and learn to understand why Threes need the attention. Knowing it's difficult for Threes to find self-worth without outside validation, Ones can practice giving them grace and compassion. Threes need to learn how to love themselves apart from the image they portray. Both Types benefit from more emotional connection and relaxation, and by simply being together.

TYPE ONE & TYPE FOUR

STRENGTHS	CHALLENGES
• Passionate	• Feelings of unworthiness
• Love beauty and kindness	• Notice flaws in each other
• Idealistic	• Controlling

LOVING IN HARMONY

Ones and Fours usually come together through their shared sense of idealism and search for a higher purpose. This couple seeks beauty, order, and love in the world. They share an arrow on the Enneagram map, which means that, if they're willing, they can balance out each other's blind spots and enhance each other's strengths. Ones' natural inclination toward stability and rational thinking attracts Fours, who need stability and reliability in relationships. Ones help Fours move toward action and strengthen their accountability because Ones are able to prioritize much better than Fours. They are more logical and will do what needs to get done regardless of how they feel. Fours bring creativity and emotional awareness to the relationship, which helps Ones discover their deeper desires and access a wider range of emotions.

CHALLENGES

These two Types see the world from different ends of the emotional spectrum, so this is where most of their challenges will manifest. Fours are emotionally intense and crave having that kind of connection with their partners. Ones can't easily access their feelings, however, making it difficult for them to meet Fours at their emotional level. Consequently, Fours feel misunderstood, unseen, and rejected, leading Ones to believe that something is wrong with them, that Fours consider them unable to be "good."

CONFLICT RESOLUTION

Ones need to adapt and accept Fours' deep emotions and quickly shifting moods. They need to practice being patient and compassionate to Fours' sensitivities. This will help Fours trust that Ones are not going to abandon them. Fours need to practice staying in the present, away from looking for what could be going wrong, and allow themselves to fully enjoy the love that they are feeling at that moment in their relationship.

TYPE ONE & TYPE FIVE

STRENGTHS
- Value personal freedom
- Rational and objective
- Witty sense of humor

CHALLENGES
- Lack of emotional connection
- Silent and controlling
- Superiority complex

LOVING IN HARMONY

This couple is attracted to each other's similar approach to life. They both have strong opinions and beliefs, and value the truth. They pursue respect and authority but also appreciate each other's calm presence. They don't like drama or strong sentiments. They bond and connect over intellectual conversation, common interests, and clever humor. Ones and Fives make steady partners for each other. They both thrive when others are not overly dependent on them, which makes their union perfect. Fives are able to recharge their energy without offending Ones, and Ones are able to keep their autonomy because Fives are quite self-reliant.

CHALLENGES

Ones and Fives have a mutual understanding of each other's needs, but problems can arise when communication begins to dwindle. If Fives retreat without letting Ones know, Ones might take this behavior as a sign of criticism or indifference. Fives retreat even further if Ones become intrusive or demanding, which will, in turn, make Ones frustrated and angry. If the other needs something, it's unlikely they will turn to each other unless absolutely necessary.

CONFLICT RESOLUTION

This pair needs to work on communication. Both of them need to speak about their feelings so that the other is aware of their emotional status. Fives can practice softening criticism toward Ones, and Ones can practice being open to Fives' ideas.

TYPE ONE & TYPE SIX

STRENGTHS
- Loyal and honorable
- Supportive and warm
- Perseverant and steadfast

CHALLENGES
- Prone to guilt
- Hard on themselves
- Highly reactive in conflict

LOVING IN HARMONY

Ones and Sixes in love are a wonderful blend of loyalty and faithfulness. They admire each other for their strong work ethic, their tendency to see the good in others, and their ability to persevere through difficult times. This couple knows they can rely on each other through thick and thin, and will be unwavering about doing the right thing. This relationship is usually built on faith and understanding that the outside world needs them to be an example of wholesome values. Ones are attracted to Sixes for their warmth and compassionate hearts; Sixes appreciate Ones' ability to make smart decisions and put them into action. They both follow through on promises and have a desire to help the world. This couple is stable and deeply committed.

CHALLENGES

This couple's sense of security wavers when they're under stress, which occurs when they take on too many commitments. Ones are critical, judgmental, and harsh toward Sixes. Sixes become defensive and will distance themselves from Ones in order to avoid being criticized. Eventually, Sixes will lash out when too much tension and resentment builds. This will aggravate Ones, who will eventually lash out in anger.

CONFLICT RESOLUTION

For this couple, it's best that Sixes practice being direct with Ones before problems arise. Sixes should resist blaming and projecting their fears onto Ones. Instead of jumping to conclusions, Sixes can ask Ones questions and try to understand the reality of the situation. Ones need to understand how anxious it makes Sixes feel when they don't feel safe with Ones' volatile anger. They both need to talk to each other as a way of not letting the tension build.

TYPE ONE & TYPE SEVEN

STRENGTHS
- Excel at making things happen
- Future-oriented
- Value their freedom

CHALLENGES
- Can be self-righteous
- Demanding and impatient
- Rationalize their behavior

LOVING IN HARMONY

Their contrasting natures bring Ones and Sevens together. This couple enjoys the balance they bring to their strengths and weaknesses. They offer each other important qualities the other may be lacking. Ones bring practicality; Sevens bring spontaneity. If they're open-minded and can see the value that the other brings, this pair can be extremely good for each other. Ones are enamored by Sevens' adventurous spirit and positive outlook. They are drawn to Sevens via their Security Lines, allowing themselves to take on the carefree nature of Sevens, to perhaps indulge in joy and play. Sevens encourage Ones to explore their desires; Ones help Sevens get focused and face their responsibilities. Ones remain steady, which helps Sevens become more grounded and levelheaded. With a bit of balance and compromise, this couple can have a truly fulfilling relationship.

CHALLENGES

Things can get messy between these two when tensions rise. Sevens get frustrated and feel stifled by Ones' need for constant perfection; they can end up feeling disconnected from Ones and may even rebel against them. Meanwhile, Ones view this behavior as childish and irresponsible. If this dynamic continues, Ones become fed up with Sevens' behavior and Sevens might be inclined to find freedom and happiness elsewhere.

CONFLICT RESOLUTION

Ones need to be less controlling and realize the beauty in what Sevens have to offer. If they're able to find grace in Sevens' imperfections, it will help them to extend that grace to themselves, which will soften their need for control. Sevens can learn a great deal from Ones' strengths. They need to practice becoming more self-disciplined and aware of Ones' needs, as well as their own.

TYPE ONE & TYPE EIGHT

STRENGTHS
- Balance of logic and emotion
- Self-reliant and strong
- Stand up for each other

CHALLENGES
- Suppressed and explosive anger
- All-or-nothing thinking
- Difficulty being vulnerable

LOVING IN HARMONY

Ones and Eights join the fight for justice with the drive to do and be good, making them a very strong and dynamic couple. Their aligned interests usually bring them together. They most often have a lot of respect and admiration for one another and will see eye to eye on a variety of topics. They enjoy spending time together, going over plans of action or ways to combine their strong forces for the good of humanity. Ones will be fired up and inspired by Eights' self-confidence and the way they go after what they want. Ones will likely attempt to adopt some of these characteristics since they're different from their own self-restraining ways. Eights can have difficulty trusting others, but in their relationship with Ones, trust is usually built right away. They're able to see Ones' integrity and feel safe enough to let down their guard. Although these two are not overly sentimental, they will show their love through acts of kindness and consideration.

CHALLENGES

Ones and Eights are obstinate, strong-willed, and demanding. They are also both in the Body Center (also known as the Instinctual Center), which means they're inclined to feel anger or rage. Eights will not want to feel controlled by Ones or inhibited by their high morals. Ones will find Eights' aggressive and impulsive nature rude and unattractive. Their anger and their need to be right can leave these two unwilling to compromise.

CONFLICT RESOLUTION

In order to resolve conflicts, this couple needs to practice patience and staying open to the other's point of view. They will have to put aside their need to be right and seek forgiveness in each other. They both benefit from exploring their emotions with one another and allowing the other to become vulnerable. Remembering their softer side will help alleviate any tense moments between these two.

TYPE ONE & TYPE NINE

STRENGTHS
- Value harmony and peace
- Enjoy being of service to others
- Kindhearted and great listeners

CHALLENGES
- Disconnected from emotions
- Tendency to stonewall
- Suppress needs

LOVING IN HARMONY

Ones and Nines are a blend of harmony and altruism. They both strive for a life that is rooted in shared values and set up for comfort. They have the ability to help one another with their shortcomings.

Typically, this couple falls in love over the idea that they can bring out the best in each other. They realize quite quickly that they share several positive characteristics, one of which is their hospitable and generous spirit. Ones fall in love with Nines' gentle nature. They often feel calm and accepted right away by Nines. As a result, Ones feel at ease with Nines and are able to soften their firm nature. Nines are attracted to the way Ones go into action with a clear and steady mind. With the same sense of purpose, this couple will bring out the best in each other.

CHALLENGES

The downfall for this couple is the different ways they react to stress. They occupy opposite ends of the emotional spectrum. Ones become contemptuous and angry. Nines, on the other hand, retreat during conflict and avoid Ones at all costs. They both will become increasingly disconnected and isolated if they are unable to treat each other with compassion.

CONFLICT RESOLUTION

This couple is in the Body Center (Instinctual Center), so anger is a strong emotion for both of them, even though it shows up in contrasting ways. It's critical that these two learn what makes the other one angry and find compromises to avoid triggering that emotion. Ones need to practice being more accepting; Nines need to learn how to face conflict in a direct, healthy manner.

TYPE TWO & TYPE TWO

STRENGTHS
- Affectionate and nurturing
- Deeply intimate
- Acutely aware of the other's needs

CHALLENGES
- Trouble receiving help
- Resentful when needs are not met
- Emotionally manipulative

LOVING IN HARMONY

Relationships mean everything to Twos, so when they come together, they are on a mission to bring love and affection to each other. They share an ardent appreciation for the way they are attentive to each other's needs and desires. This pairing enjoys the language of love and is comfortable being vulnerable; they're both able to reveal their feelings without a moment's hesitation. They connect quickly and develop a deep understanding of their similarities. What makes this a successful couple is their willingness to work hard at creating a fulfilling relationship for each other.

CHALLENGES

This couple can easily fall into codependent patterns. A common situation occurs when either of them starts relying on the other to bring happiness and a sense of fulfillment. Twos struggle with being able to express their needs to each other or let the other know when a particular need is not being met. When they feel rejected or underappreciated, they'll either retreat or push harder to get the other to need them.

CONFLICT RESOLUTION

It is vital to the success of the relationship that Twos develop their own sense of self. They need to practice developing their independence to begin to feel whole on their own. To that end, both of them should spend plenty of time alone to reflect and check in with their own emotions and needs. If Twos tend to their own needs as much as they can, they will enjoy a happy and fulfilling relationship.

TYPE TWO & TYPE THREE

STRENGTHS
- Charming and flirtatious
- Ability to read the other well
- Highly supportive

CHALLENGES
- Seek outside approval
- Lack of self-worth
- Suffer from feelings of shame

LOVING IN HARMONY

Twos and Threes are both optimistic. People are attracted to them by their incredible interpersonal skills—which is probably what drew this couple together in the first place. They're extremely supportive of each other and have a deep understanding of what the other needs. Twos enjoy expressing their love through compliments, and Threes love to hear them. This couple also values living a fulfilling life. Together, they make a magnetic couple.

CHALLENGES

One of the overall themes for this pairing is that they thrive on appreciation and applause. If either one of them begins to feel as though they're not getting enough of that, tensions quickly escalate. Twos tend to give too much of themselves and neglect their own needs in order to receive love and appreciation. If Twos don't receive it, they become emotionally manipulative and domineering. If Threes do not receive admiration for all their efforts, they throw themselves into even more work while disconnecting from their emotions.

CONFLICT RESOLUTION

It's important that this couple develops a strong sense of their self-worth based on who they are, rather than what they do. Threes need to practice balancing work and their relationships; Twos should develop independence and a sense of fulfillment outside of their relationship. Both of them value being in a loving and affirming relationship. If either of them begins to feel neglected or unappreciated, they should deal with these feelings before they lead to tension or conflict.

TYPE TWO & TYPE FOUR

STRENGTHS
- Enjoy sharing their feelings
- Relish in deep and meaningful conversations
- Relationship-oriented

CHALLENGES
- Highly sensitive
- Fear of abandonment
- Tend to become codependent

LOVING IN HARMONY

A deep emotional connection usually draws these Types together. Both of them operate from the Heart Center (also known as the Feeling Center), which means they view life and love quite similarly. They're open and honest with each other and can talk for days on end about how they feel. They allow each other limitless ways to be vulnerable and authentic. This couple is able to connect on deeper and more profound levels than with any other Types. Twos are drawn to Fours' sensitivity, compassion, and mysterious ways. They're intrigued but simultaneously enamored. Fours love it when Twos give them all of their attention and focus. Fours see in Twos the ability to take action, which makes them feel more confident just being in their presence.

CHALLENGES

Their strong emotional kinship can actually create occasional issues for these two. They never stop craving intimacy and connection, making it difficult to be objective or logical. Being immersed in their emotions will prompt the majority of their arguments; when under stress, either of them can become emotionally volatile. Twos can experience Fours' dramatics as self-absorption; Fours feel smothered by Twos or irritated by what they perceive as their phoniness. At some point, they will both feel as though the other is too needy.

CONFLICT RESOLUTION

Twos can practice their emotional honesty with Fours—if there's anyone to learn that skill with, it's Fours! In order for Twos to access their true emotions, they need to spend quality time away to process and connect with themselves. Fours need to practice focusing on the positive as well as modulating their emotional intensities.

TYPE TWO & TYPE FIVE

STRENGTHS
- Opposites attract
- Balancing logic and emotions
- Teach each other different ways to love

CHALLENGES
- Different communication styles
- Polarized set of needs
- Challenging differences

LOVING IN HARMONY

Twos paired with Fives is a classic tale of opposites attracting. What one lacks, the other has a strength in, and vice versa. The initial spark between these two might be quite intense and extreme. They'll both notice right away that they have differences, but will choose to throw caution to the wind and ignore them. Twos are attracted to Fives for their emotional composure; Fives, usually out of sheer curiosity, eventually give in to Twos' persuasive ways. It makes sense that Twos would pursue Fives, who are quite emotionally reserved and quiet— but it could go either way. This couple, if emotionally healthy, can balance out each other beautifully and share a wonderful bond of commitment and love.

CHALLENGES
There are so many differences between these two Types that they can become overwhelming. Fives need a lot of personal space and will erect boundaries for themselves. They might inadvertently reject Twos by being reclusive and emotionally detached. Conversely, Twos may feel resentful toward Fives for not meeting their needs, withholding their nurturing and loving side.

CONFLICT RESOLUTION
This couple will have to practice open communication in order to avoid assumptions and misunderstandings. For their communication to be effective, they'll need to practice a few things: Twos need to learn how to process their emotions without getting worked up, since this will only alienate Fives; Fives need to be more compassionate toward Twos by accepting and discussing their feelings. With ample communication and understanding, this relationship could be a wonderful opportunity for emotional growth and healing.

TYPE TWO & TYPE SIX

STRENGTHS
- Devoted and loyal
- Family-oriented
- Enjoy being of service

CHALLENGES
- Codependency
- Overly accommodating
- Difficulty making decisions

LOVING IN HARMONY
Twos and Sixes have the potential to be a lovely pairing. Both of these Types want to feel safe and cared for; luckily for them, that's a quality they find in each other. They both value supporting one another (as well as close friends and family) through trying times. They are readily available to lend a helping hand to those in need. Sometimes their generosity is extended into their community. Twos really appreciate Sixes' loyalty to themselves as well as to their family. This is especially

important if Twos aren't particularly close with their own families. Sixes are attracted to Twos' warmth, openheartedness, and compassion for others. As with most people, Sixes may be hesitant to trust, but when Twos' authenticity is revealed, Sixes feel right at home.

CHALLENGES

Twos may not like how mistrustful and suspicious Sixes can be. They can become annoyed by Sixes' constant questioning and testing of their motivations, which may eventually lead to accusations and arguments. This is Sixes' way of testing the loyalty of those they are close to. Twos have a tendency to become dependent and emotionally needy. This might endear Sixes at times, but Twos' need for so much attention will eventually wear on Sixes' nerves. They may feel Twos' need for attention is intrusive and begin to withdraw. This will likely trigger Twos' fear of rejection, and they will also begin to withdraw.

CONFLICT RESOLUTION

Twos need to understand that Sixes' questioning their loyalty and suspicions come from a fear of abandonment. They should practice stating what they need and want and allowing Sixes to express their fears without taking them personally. Sixes need to try owning their fears and effectively communicating them without projecting them onto Twos.

TYPE TWO & TYPE SEVEN

STRENGTHS
- Enjoy making others feel loved
- Love having a good time
- Skilled at creating a positive environment

CHALLENGES
- Emotional and overdramatic
- Avoid negative emotions
- Feelings of superiority

LOVING IN HARMONY

Twos and Sevens are brought together by their bubbly nature and joyful heart. They're attracted to the other's charismatic smile and gusto for life. Twos and Sevens have lots of energy and positivity, and they enjoy indulging in the richness that life brings. Twos are attracted to Sevens' adventurous and playful spirit; it allows them to join in on the lighthearted fun. Sevens are attracted to Twos' depth of emotion and selfless character; it reminds them that there's beauty and meaning in all kinds of feelings (not just positive ones).

CHALLENGES

These two will have lots of fun together, but problems may arise when the fun stops and the unpleasant realities of life settle in. Twos need more intimacy and stability than Sevens care to give. Sevens want and very much need their freedom. They do not like to be tied down or committed—which is the opposite of what Twos are looking for. Sevens may interpret Twos' need for emotional connections as a way of "guilt-tripping" or "manipulating" them.

CONFLICT RESOLUTION

Twos need intimacy and connection. Sevens need to try experiencing the full range of emotions with Twos. If they truly commit to Twos and dig deeper into their emotions, Sevens may find that they'll be enriching all of their shared experiences. Twos need to practice developing their independence and pursuing interests outside of their relationship, which will build their self-confidence as well.

TYPE TWO & TYPE EIGHT

STRENGTHS
- Protective and loyal
- Generous and supportive
- Powerful sexual chemistry

CHALLENGES
- Easily angered and controlling
- Possessive and manipulative
- Difficulty respecting boundaries

LOVING IN HARMONY
This couple embodies the feminine (Twos) and masculine (Eights) energies. Twos are attracted to Eights' strength, self-confidence, and passion; Eights are enamored of Twos' compassionate heart and nurturing nature. This couple is a blend of strength and generosity, and will likely have a strong sexual chemistry. They have the ability to complement each other's strengths and weaknesses if they're sufficiently open-minded about the process.

CHALLENGES
Twos are focused on their interpersonal relationships and very much want to be the center of Eights' world. Eights also want to be the center of Twos' world but in a more independent way. Twos may try to soften Eights' heart, but Eights, seeing this as manipulative, may become aggressive and dismissive of Twos' efforts. Twos can be easily hurt by Eights' behavior and may begin to think of them as cruel.

CONFLICT RESOLUTION
Twos need to practice being direct and forthcoming when speaking to Eights. Eights will appreciate their honesty and may encourage Twos to embody their inner power. Eights need to learn how to control their anger in healthier ways. When they find the proper outlet for their powerful energy, they're more likely to bring empowerment and kindness to the relationship.

TYPE TWO & TYPE NINE

STRENGTHS
- Value harmony and peace
- Enjoy being of service to others
- Kindhearted and great listeners

CHALLENGES
- Disconnected from emotions
- Tendency to stonewall
- Suppress their needs

LOVING IN HARMONY

Twos and Nines are relationship-oriented. They're both attracted to each other's need for harmony. Twos can be just as sensitive as Nines, and Nines can be equally as caring and nurturing as Twos. This loving and warm couple are also incredibly supportive and accommodating to each other. Twos are drawn to Nines' gentle manner and easygoing and calm nature, especially during troubled times. They usually feel instantly safe and accepted by Nines. Nines are attracted to Twos' charm and energy. Together, this couple embodies sensitivity and kindness. They both strive to make each other happy.

CHALLENGES

These Types can run into serious problems making decisions as a unit and figuring out who's going to take the lead. They can both be quite indecisive. On top of that, Twos don't care for conflict and Nines are incredibly averse to it. It will most likely be Twos who step up to the plate to figure things out. But it will come at a cost—eventually, Twos will overextend themselves in order to keep the relationship in harmony for Nines.

CONFLICT RESOLUTION

This couple shares a One Wing, which means they will need to work through some anger issues. Although Nines are averse to conflict, their anger comes out in a passive-aggressive manner; Twos usually boil over with an anger that can be volatile. Nines will need to practice setting goals and priorities for themselves—as well as boundaries for others—when they are feeling pressured by Twos to make a decision. Twos need to eventually accept that Nines are resistant to change, but not incapable of it. They should practice being patient and let Nines develop their assertiveness without pressuring them.

TYPE THREE & TYPE THREE

STRENGTHS
- Value accomplishment
- Charming and sociable
- Attractive and charismatic

CHALLENGES
- Inability to compromise
- Several insecurities
- Opportunistic tendencies

LOVING IN HARMONY
By society's standards, Threes are usually very attractive and have winning personalities. It's no surprise that this couple is usually brought together because they like what they see. Threes have more than just looks, though. They are hard workers, high-achieving, and goal oriented. When they find these qualities in someone else, they will feel as though they have struck gold. They're going to have a deeper understanding than most about how they approach the world and their desire to be the best. They have what it takes to work well as a team and have no problems gushing over each other's success. The sky is the limit for these two if they are physically and emotionally healthy and willing to make compromises along the way.

CHALLENGES
The biggest obstacle that this couple may face is if their goals go out of alignment. Their once supportive and encouraging partners will withdraw in order to continue on with their respective goals. These two may develop an unhealthy competitive attitude toward each other. Threes tend to be out of touch with their emotions, making

it difficult for them to communicate how they're feeling about each other and their relationship issues.

CONFLICT RESOLUTION

Threes must learn the value of intimacy within the relationship. They will have to work separately on developing emotional connections to themselves first, and then on allowing themselves to express these feelings to each other. During conflict, it is important (especially for Threes) to be able to convey how a particular situation is making them feel rather than how it's affecting their image. Encouraging each other to practice emotional availability will bring them closer together and strengthen their bond.

TYPE THREE & TYPE FOUR

STRENGTHS
- Romantic and passionate
- Complementing strengths
- Creative and intense

CHALLENGES
- Need constant validation and approval
- Contrasting core values
- Image-conscious

LOVING IN HARMONY

Threes focus their energy on achieving success and getting outside validation, whereas Fours are concerned about cultivating beauty, having emotional depth, and creating a unique, authentic identity. Although this pairing approaches the world through very different lenses, they can offer each other several opportunities for growth when they are both operating from a higher state of awareness. Threes show Fours how to move into action and be efficient, encouraging them to reach their full potential. Fours offer Threes the language of emotions and the value of authenticity. This couple embodies strength balanced with opportunity for growth.

CHALLENGES

Threes can quickly become irritated and annoyed by Fours' temperamental moods and their inability to be as productive and efficient as they are. They also become impatient and irritated when Fours are not proactive about working on their personal and relationship goals. Fours will find Threes to be phony, too concerned with their image, and lacking in emotional depth. They'll begin to withdraw, feel rejected if Threes throw themselves into work, and eventually become hostile and demand attention.

CONFLICT RESOLUTION

Threes need to come to the realization that in order to have a healthy and happy relationship with Fours, they need to slow down their pace for progress and success, open their hearts to show Fours their true feelings, and commit to making the relationship a priority. Fours will need to bend a little too, in order to meet Threes halfway. They can practice sticking to their goals, staying in the present, and realizing that they also need attention and validation.

TYPE THREE & TYPE FIVE

STRENGTHS
- Common values
- Perseverance and independence
- Highly competent and emotionally contained

CHALLENGES
- Overly competitive
- Lack of interest in each other
- Emotionally disconnected

LOVING IN HARMONY

This pairing has a lot in common and shares many of the same core values. Threes are outgoing and charismatic, and have strong interpersonal skills. Fives find these traits, along with Threes' self-confidence and competence, very attractive. Threes will immediately be attracted to Fives' insightfulness and competency. Stimulated by one another's knowledge and expertise in their chosen fields, they also appreciate each other's need for space and independence. This couple may feel as though they have found a wonderful and complementary match for themselves.

CHALLENGES

These two share similarities in the issues that could do harm to the relationship. Both of them place a lot of emphasis on their work and can inadvertently forget about each other's needs. They are also very stimulated by each other mentally. Intimacy may be lacking due to these Types both being very independent with seemingly low emotional needs, which can eventually lead to emotional detachment over time.

CONFLICT RESOLUTION

This couple will need to schedule time for dates, romance, and emotional connection. It doesn't have to be elaborate, just meaningful and intentional in order for them to open their hearts to each other. They might even find it useful to learn how to do this at a retreat or through a counselor. It will be overwhelming for both of them to take this emotional leap, but it will be absolutely necessary for the sake of the relationship.

TYPE THREE & TYPE SIX

STRENGTHS
- Productive and practical
- Respectful and admiring
- Shared fundamental values

CHALLENGES
- Low levels of awareness
- Tend to be workaholics
- Need for external reassurance

LOVING IN HARMONY

This couple is willing to go the distance and has a lot of potential to form a loving and supportive union. Threes are attracted to the warmth and concern Sixes offer, and Sixes appreciates Threes for their positive mindset and sparkling personality. They are practical, diplomatic, and very personable. Sixes are buoyed by Threes' encouraging spirit, and Threes appreciate Sixes' insight. This couple values not only the opinions of their friends and family, but their attachment to them as well. They can have a secure and loyal connection.

CHALLENGES

Threes can be inconsiderate and not the best listeners, especially under stress. They have a tendency to come off as dismissive as well. This will cause Sixes to doubt Threes' loyalty and to become anxious. Sixes are overly cautious and can procrastinate a great deal before being able to make a decision. Threes will be frustrated by this behavior and may badger Sixes in order to get things done. The cycle of impatience and indecision will become the point of contention between them. Eventually, they will have to deal with the repression of these main issues.

CONFLICT RESOLUTION

Threes need to accept that Sixes do not have the same natural self-confidence that they do. Sixes need time to process situations; they can't make spontaneous decisions the way Threes do. Threes need to start by respecting this about Sixes, and practice using tact and empathy. Sixes need to see that Threes have a set of coping mechanisms that make it difficult to connect with them. Sixes should practice how to be clear about their feelings and their opinions without pushing Threes away with accusatory questions.

TYPE THREE & TYPE SEVEN

STRENGTHS
- Energetic go-getters
- Optimistic and fun-loving
- Uplifting and encouraging

CHALLENGES
- Not good at listening or focusing
- Tend to take too many risks
- Avoid uncomfortable emotions

LOVING IN HARMONY

What this couple may lack in modesty, they make up for in energy! Threes and Sevens are quite possibly the Types with the most vitality. They have much in common in how they approach life. Threes are attracted to Sevens' fun-loving and spontaneous ways, which perfectly complement their outgoing personality. Sevens love how charming and successful Threes are; they admire how willing and determined Threes are to achieve their dreams. This couple combines adventure, drive, and an insatiable lust for a well-lived life.

CHALLENGES

Since both these Types are self-focused, they have a tendency to fall into selfish patterns. They can both be stubborn and uncompromising around their own desires. Neither of them wants to deal with negative emotions or problems in their relationship. This will cause several issues to be swept under the rug and not dealt with until one of them calls out the other about it. They value their priorities to a fault and will likely place them above the relationship if they see fit.

CONFLICT RESOLUTION

Threes and Sevens struggle with feelings of anxiety when their lives slow down; when their minds and bodies are still, that's when emotions arise. Threes and Sevens don't want to deal with their emotions. Sevens are afraid of emotions because they're afraid of the pain; Threes can be unaware of emotions altogether. This couple will need to work on processing their own feelings, including painful ones they may encounter within the relationship.

TYPE THREE & TYPE EIGHT

STRENGTHS
- Passionate and fierce
- Supportive and grounded
- Self-confident and ambitious

CHALLENGES
- Guarded
- Jealous and possessive
- Controlling and blunt

LOVING IN HARMONY

This is quite a fearsome couple. They both bring power, assertiveness, and success to each other in different ways. These traits are what attracts them to each other. Threes like how Eights don't care much about what people think and just go after what they want. This inspires Threes to embrace who they are rather than what people think they are. Eights gravitate toward the self-confidence and success of Threes. They like that Threes are kind and generous, yet not overly sentimental (which in turn helps Threes build trust). These two have a lot of charisma and ambition. Together, they have the capability of being very influential and will stop at nothing to impress and succeed.

CHALLENGES

Control and trust issues can put stress on this relationship. Neither of these two likes to be told what to do. Threes have a hard time showing who they really are because they fear rejection. Eights want to see the real person underneath the mask. Threes are very charming, but Eights may interpret that behavior to mean that Threes can't be trusted. Eights tend to be jealous. Threes will not appreciate Eights' control tactics and they don't want to be confronted. These differences could lead to them throwing themselves into their work. Eights might withdraw their support, leaving Threes feeling unappreciated.

If trust is not built or goals are not aligned, these two will have a difficult time together.

CONFLICT RESOLUTION

This couple will need to practice being vulnerable with one another in order to establish a strong bond and create trust. They both want and need to feel supported, so it's up to them to find a way to build on each other's strengths. Eights need to provide Threes with more compassion and encouragement; Threes need to practice always being honest, up-front, and genuine with Eights. Once Eights know they can trust Threes, they will be more emotionally available.

TYPE THREE & TYPE NINE

STRENGTHS
- Pleasant and likable
- Seek comfort and security
- Balance out each other's strengths

CHALLENGES
- Tendency to people-please
- Stubborn standoffs
- Avoid relationship issues

LOVING IN HARMONY

Threes and Nines are highly idealistic, friendly, and supportive of each other. They bring balance to what the other needs. They share common values and goals, making it easier to plan for the future. Neither of them likes to argue and both find comfort in routine. Nines are attracted to Threes' unwavering energy; they admire the way they get things done. Threes appreciate Nines' ability to make them feel accepted and loved for who they are. When this couple is in sync, they can be incredibly good for each other.

CHALLENGES

Their personal challenges stress and frustrate each other. Threes can be quite impatient with Nines' slow pace and lack of priorities. Nines feel rejected by Threes' flustered attitude toward them and may retreat and perhaps move even slower through passive-aggressive behaviors. Nines will be disheartened by Threes' inability to slow down from work or goal-setting, leaving little time for tending to the relationship. They both avoid conflict and will need to address issues if they want to stop the distancing.

CONFLICT RESOLUTION

Threes need to understand that, although Nines appreciate Threes for their hard work and commitment to goals, it's not what they love about them. Nines love people for who they are. Threes need to practice being themselves around Nines, and allowing them into their emotional world, little by little. For Nines, it's all about developing their voice and self-direction so that they don't completely merge with Threes. They need to practice more self-awareness and build mindfulness to fight their tendency to allow outside forces and people to decide everything for them.

TYPE FOUR & TYPE FOUR

STRENGTHS

- Deeply connected to their emotions
- Romantics and idealists
- Sensitive to each other's needs

CHALLENGES

- Over-idealize their relationship
- Fear of abandonment
- Jealousy and control issues

LOVING IN HARMONY

Like other double pairings, these two highly individual souls have a deep rapport with each other. They're so used to feeling misunderstood that when they find each other, it will feel as though they were meant to be; they finally will feel a sense of kinship with someone else. Fours recognize emotional depth and are not scared or thrown off by the intensity. They love sharing their hearts and minds, and enjoy finding meaning in just about anything. They also understand the way their emotions often fluctuate and can accept each other without question or judgment. It's quite possible that this highly creative couple will feel as if they have found their soulmate.

CHALLENGES

Fear of abandonment keeps this couple pushing and pulling each other away. They may have frequent arguments over unmet expectations and desires. Their idealized notions that the other is perfect will soon melt away, leaving a perfectly flawed human—and that might be too much for them to accept. They may become disenchanted with each other and begin to feel that nothing ever turns out the way they want it to. They'll start to think they aren't worthy of happiness. Sometimes such strong emotional intensity can cause them to separate.

CONFLICT RESOLUTION

They will need to become aware of how much they're idealizing their significant other. As much as both of them want to be everything to each other, they need to accept that in order to feel whole and happy, they need to practice staying grateful for all that they have and everything wonderful their partner brings. They both should also focus on steadying their emotions by exercising and being in nature.

TYPE FOUR & TYPE FIVE

STRENGTHS
- Unconventional and quirky
- Cherish their time alone
- Stimulating conversation

CHALLENGES
- Conflicting levels of emotion
- Sense of not belonging
- Social awkwardness

LOVING IN HARMONY

This unconventional couple shares several similarities as well as opposites that strengthen what the other is lacking. They thrive off of creativity, curiosity, and living in their imaginations. Fours offer Fives an invitation to go beyond their thoughts into a colorful world of emotions. Fives show Fours ways to be more logical and grounded. This couple usually spends their time together creating, exploring, or having lively conversations at their favorite artisanal coffee shop. Both of them appreciate each other's quirks and individuality, allowing them to be completely themselves.

CHALLENGES

This couple has contrasting emotional needs—this is where they will struggle to find a satisfying balance. Fours need a lot of attention, which can quickly overwhelm Fives, who may become drained and off-put by such neediness. Fives are emotionally detached and can often come across as cold and unavailable to Fours. If the connection is not made, Fours will get caught in a cycle of trying to connect and feeling rejected; Fives will want more space away from Fours to avoid this cycle.

CONFLICT RESOLUTION

This couple will need to establish trust and some degree of intimacy in order to truly understand and have compassion for where the other is coming from. Fives value their privacy and can get easily overwhelmed with too much emotion. Fours need to respect their boundaries and can practice easing their emotions and fears. Fives need to practice gradually staying connected over time, having confidence that relationships can be nurturing, and appreciating Fours' depth of feeling and deep well of empathy.

TYPE FOUR & TYPE SIX

STRENGTHS
- Warmth and humor
- Emotionally supportive
- Purposeful and well-meaning

CHALLENGES
- Insecure and self-doubting
- Emotional outbursts
- Inclined to imagine the worst

LOVING IN HARMONY

This couple connects over genuineness and warmth. They share several similarities as well as several insecurities, which allows them to easily understand each other's worlds. Fours and Sixes can be highly empathetic, providing each other with the support and security the other needs. Fours enjoy Sixes' quick wit and like bantering with them, which brings out the playful spirit of Fours. Sixes are attracted to Fours' creativity; they are also intrigued by the sense of mystery that surrounds Fours. Together, they feel loved and valued.

CHALLENGES

This couple struggles with a fear of being abandoned. They can both spiral into a cycle of mistrust and create a constant push and pull between each other. They both have vulnerabilities that lead to feelings of rejection. Sixes mistrust Fours' unpredictable mood; Sixes' perceptual habit of worry and doubt will have Fours feeling a lack of excitement when they're unable to move past Sixes' fears. During conflict, both can be highly reactive and emotionally intense, which can sometimes be overreactions on both their parts.

CONFLICT RESOLUTION

Fours need to understand that Sixes' fears are deeply rooted; Sixes can feel supported if they share with Fours the fears and anxieties that trigger them. Sixes need to realize that Fours' emotional intensity just needs to be expressed—it's not a problem that they have to solve. Fours want to be heard and understood too. This couple benefits greatly from simply listening to each other's concerns and not judging them.

TYPE FOUR & TYPE SEVEN

STRENGTHS

- Creative and imaginative
- Love interesting conversation
- Help each other come alive

CHALLENGES

- Overly self-involved
- Impatient
- Have several opposing values

LOVING IN HARMONY

This couple is the epitome of opposites attract! Their strengths complement each other's challenges. They share common approaches to the world: They're both looking for variety, enjoying special experiences, and having fascinating conversations. Fours are attracted to Sevens' adventurous and carefree spirit. It makes them feel alive and allows them to have more fun than they normally would have. Sevens are intrigued by Fours' emotional depth; if Sevens allow it, Fours can help them discover the full range of human emotions. This relationship can be very successful if both Fours and Sevens are open to understanding themselves more.

CHALLENGES

What brings them together also has the potential to create stress and anger between them. Fours will not appreciate Sevens' intolerance of negative emotions, their dismissiveness when they are in an avoidant mode, and their insensitivity to their and others' emotions. Sevens may conclude that Fours' emotional depth hinders their freedom and happiness. Sevens don't want to be limited by anything, especially by the darker emotions of life. These fundamental issues will need to be addressed early on in the relationship.

CONFLICT RESOLUTION

Sevens need to acknowledge and become aware of their avoidance of negative emotions. Both these Types need to practice exploring their feelings, staying in the moment, and finding gratitude and peace within themselves there. They can work on appreciating the lighter and darker sides of life together. Connection and commitment are important components of their relationship. They bring a tremendous amount of value to the other; they'll just need to work on appreciating it.

TYPE FOUR & TYPE EIGHT

STRENGTHS
- Value truth and authenticity
- Intuitive powers
- Highly expressive

CHALLENGES
- Strong-willed
- Jealous and possessive
- Controlling and resistant

LOVING IN HARMONY

The passion between these two is intense. Fours and Eights share some of the same strengths, such as their ability to easily express themselves, their commitment to the truth, and their strong convictions. This couple can also be quite provocative and might enjoy indulging in a little drama. Fours are attracted to the way Eights command a room with their mere presence. They like how Eights come across as authentic—this helps Fours see them for who they truly are. At first, Eights are intrigued by Fours' mysteriousness; in time, they come to respect them for their individuality. This pairing helps both parties come alive.

CHALLENGES

Control issues will bring both of these Types to confrontation. Fours are afraid of being abandoned and rejected; Eights are afraid of being controlled and manipulated, especially through emotion. Under stress, this couple will inadvertently provoke each other, and because they're both incredibly intense, they will find themselves in highly reactive states. Fours don't appreciate how domineering Eights can be; Eights will fight against Fours' volatile emotions.

CONFLICT RESOLUTION

As they process their intense emotions, this couple will need to practice seeing what's really beneath their arguments. They need to come out of a reactionary state in order to actually resolve their issues. Because Eights may feel manipulated by their loved one's strong emotions, Fours need to practice stabilizing their emotions in order to effectively engage with their partners. Eights need to accept Fours' emotions without judgment and without resistance. This couple should practice how to embrace their own vulnerabilities, which will help them become more logical as well as more loving.

TYPE FOUR & TYPE NINE

STRENGTHS
- Highly creative
- Empathetic and friendly
- Idealistic and intuitive

CHALLENGES
- Resistant and stubborn
- Lack of self-worth
- Stagnation and inactivity

LOVING IN HARMONY

When Fours and Nines find each other, they may feel as if they have discovered their soulmate. They'll notice an immediate similarity in how they see the world, and will see that their communication styles are often complementary. These two are both creative and intuitively sense each other's needs. Fours feel safe with Nines, who are generally very accepting, warm, and nonjudgmental. Nines love how empathetic Fours can be. This soulful couple usually has a deep and intimate relationship.

CHALLENGES

Fours tend to focus on what is missing from a relationship; when they express their needs to Nines, this may come off as conflict—which Nines are usually averse to. Instead of working through the conflict, Nines tend to withdraw and may even shut down completely. This reaction may make Fours intensify their demands in order to get their needs met. This dynamic inevitably leads to an unhealthy cycle if these Types are not equipped with the resources they need to navigate these issues.

CONFLICT RESOLUTION

To resolve conflict between these two, it's important for Nines to acknowledge Fours' concerns for them to stay present while they work toward a resolution. Fours can get to a resolution faster by practicing patience with Nines and by not using judgmental or critical language to express their frustrations. By remaining calm, Nines will be more likely to express their own concerns as well. It will benefit this couple to determine their objectives before "entering the ring" of conflict resolution.

TYPE FIVE & TYPE FIVE

STRENGTHS
- Peaceful and trustworthy
- Enjoy intellectual conversation
- Comforted by the other's presence

CHALLENGES
- Experience sharp bursts of anger
- Intellectual competitiveness
- Depriving the other of emotional connection

LOVING IN HARMONY

This couple is drawn to one another on a very intellectual level. As with any double pairing, they share a deep understanding of how they relate to the world. This connection is very important for Fives, who are in observation mode a great deal of the time. Fives can simply enjoy each other's company; they feel relaxed and don't feel the need to always be talking—although they do enjoy sharing stimulating conversations and maybe even friendly debates with one another. This couple is generally not very emotional, but they can have an intensity that only they can acknowledge and appreciate.

CHALLENGES

Fives can run into issues if they disagree on the level of intimacy either one of them desires. Fives are not generally emotionally expressive and can come across as disconnected from their feelings. They also don't feel comfortable when emotional responses are expected of them. Resentment, anger, and abandonment emerge if one of the Fives in this relationship wants more than the other is willing to give. The other may be left feeling that too much is being asked of them.

CONFLICT RESOLUTION

Since some balance of emotional connection is key in any relationship, it's important for two Fives to be aware that, at times, the other person may need more attention and emotion. Both of them need to participate in keeping this relationship healthy by taking turns opening up and sharing their vulnerabilities. It might benefit this couple to practice taking turns nurturing each other, even in small ways.

TYPE FIVE & TYPE SIX

STRENGTHS
- Respect each other's boundaries
- Seek understanding and insight
- Crave honesty and accuracy

CHALLENGES
- Tend to question everything
- Major difference in emotional responsiveness
- Difficulty taking action

LOVING IN HARMONY

Fives and Sixes share not only an intellectual connection but also a natural sense of curiosity and thoughtfulness. They might even share several sensitivities. This couple values loyalty and honesty, and they are both amazing problem-solvers. Fives like how friendly and respectful Sixes can be, and Sixes appreciate how decisive and knowledgeable Fives can be. Together, this couple's bond can be a lovely mix of head and heart.

CHALLENGES

A relationship challenge that might present itself is Sixes' fear of abandonment and Fives' disconnection from the outside world. Sixes crave connection and support from their community; Fives would rather remain self-reliant, free of demands on their time, and not obligated to attend social events. Sixes may begin to feel as if they are doing everything alone, without their Five partner. This could easily trigger Sixes' fear of abandonment, which Fives may perceive as Sixes being too codependent.

CONFLICT RESOLUTION

There will have to be some compromise for both parties to feel safe. Sixes can learn how to be more self-reliant like Fives and be okay when their partner is not always right next to them. Fives can give Sixes more reassurance and even join them on select social outings.

TYPE FIVE & TYPE SEVEN

STRENGTHS
- Enjoy being intellectually stimulated
- Love sharing ideas and explorations
- Highly value their independence

CHALLENGES
- Avoid deeper emotions
- Restless energy and anxieties
- Noncommittal tendencies

LOVING IN HARMONY

This is quite an inquisitive couple. They both enjoy learning and exploring new ideas. They are both highly independent people and usually have a great sense of humor that they turn into lots of inside jokes. Sevens bring a lot of energy and a positive outlook, both of which Fives are attracted to. Sevens love how unconventional, decisive, and interesting Fives are. This couple nicely balances out each other.

CHALLENGES

Even though Fives and Sevens balance out each other's differences, those differences will, of course, be what creates conflict between them. Fives tend to be quite private and reserved; Sevens are basically an open book and have a tendency to be impulsive. Fives enjoy a fair amount of quiet time; Sevens love going out and having real-life adventures. They can begin to drift apart if they don't respect the other's desires and boundaries.

CONFLICT RESOLUTION

Fives can learn from Sevens' way of approaching the world, which Sevens see as a place of limitless possibility where they want to enjoy all that they can. Fives might think they don't have enough money, time, or energy to do those things—but they can lean into Fives' approach a little as a way of releasing some of this fear. Sevens can learn a lot about how to preserve their time, money, and energy from Fives. This can be a win-win situation if both parties are willing to try—maybe one weekend is for adventure and the next is for staying in and resting (and saving money).

TYPE FIVE & TYPE EIGHT

STRENGTHS
- Enjoy a good debate
- Value autonomy and their freedom
- Establish healthy boundaries

CHALLENGES
- Need to be right
- Overanalyzing situations
- Not in touch with their emotions

LOVING IN HARMONY

At first glance, this couple might look like an "opposites attract" situation, but Fives and Eights actually have a fair bit in common. They're both highly independent and are attracted to that feature in each other. Eights are in the Body Center (also known as the Instinctual Center) and typically have lots of self-confidence and spontaneity, which Fives find attractive. Eights can appreciate how trustworthy and dependable Fives can be, which makes Eights feel safe and grounded. This can be quite a strong and effective pairing.

CHALLENGES

One major factor that causes conflict in this couple is the very different ways they communicate with each other. Eights are typically very blunt and get right to the point. Fives will typically see this behavior as intimidating and too combative, causing them to shut down. This will only aggravate Eights, and they might become even more confrontational until they get a rise out of Fives. Arguments between this couple can become quite hostile and maybe even violent.

CONFLICT RESOLUTION

Fives, although they don't show a lot of emotion, are quite sensitive; Eights need to keep this in mind in how they approach Fives during conflict. If there is an issue that needs to be resolved, it's best if Eights take the time to calm down, so as to not be overly reactive and confrontational. Fives need to work on being able to ground themselves during disagreements and set healthy boundaries with Eights. Together, this couple can resolve conflicts with effective listening and responding.

TYPE FIVE & TYPE NINE

STRENGTHS
- Value plenty of personal space
- Patient and supportive
- Undemanding and respectful

CHALLENGES
- Withdraw into their minds
- Difficulty expressing emotions
- Avoid conflict

LOVING IN HARMONY

Things can be very harmonious between Fives and Nines. They both value their privacy, space, and energy. Neither of them feels pressured or judged by the other. When they're in a healthy zone, this pairing is quite supportive of each other's happiness. They are both peaceful beings who crave stability and someone they can share their ideas with. Fives appreciate that Nines are generally undemanding and very understanding of their quirks; Nines truly love how patient Fives are with them. This pairing can be a great mix of companionship and acceptance, which can be freeing for the both of them.

CHALLENGES

As much as they love their autonomy, too much space and time apart might cause these two to drift apart and resent each other. Fives and Nines are conflict-avoidant; when issues arise, they are both inclined to superficially "let it go." Nines typically express their anger passive-aggressively; Fives emotionally detach and become cold and distant. It's not uncommon for either of them to have an emotional outburst that finally reveals underlying problems.

CONFLICT RESOLUTION

It's imperative for these two to bring more emotional awareness to their relationship. Both need to practice opening up about how they're feeling during times of stress or discomfort so they do not suppress anger. To be better able to find resolution with their partner, Fives can check in on Nines to see where they are emotionally; Nines can practice developing more self-confidence and speaking up for themselves.

TYPE SIX & TYPE SIX

STRENGTHS
- Value commitment and trust
- Enjoy lighthearted banter
- Faithful and supportive

CHALLENGES
- Share fears of abandonment
- Anxious and reactive under stress
- Need constant reassurance

LOVING IN HARMONY

When two Sixes come together in love, there is an immediate understanding of how they cope with the outside world. They inherently relate to each other's fears and anxieties. Not only do they feel understood and truly seen, they also feel safe and more likely to drop their defenses than they would with other Types. Of course, as they share a lot of the same values, this couple will often feel as though it's them against the world, creating a very loyal and committed dynamic.

CHALLENGES

This couple will encounter a great deal of stress caused by their self-doubt and anxieties. They may also feed off of each other's stress and anxiety. They are in the reactive stance, which will make their arguments very emotional, not leaving much room for rational thinking. That's how this couple can get themselves caught up in emotional confusion and accusatory conversations. They both fear being abandoned, creating a cycle of testing the other's loyalty—which, instead of reassuring them, can erode trust altogether.

CONFLICT RESOLUTION

It's best if this couple realizes early on that there will be several moments of doubt and maybe even suspicion of the other's intentions and motives. It will be important for them to check in with each other regularly to establish a stable and comforting space for them to voice their concerns without the other feeling attacked or defensive. They should practice acknowledging and celebrating their positive experiences with each other. They also should learn what soothes each other's anxieties, because it will probably be different for both of them.

TYPE SIX & TYPE SEVEN

STRENGTHS
- Encourage each other's strengths
- Curious and quick-thinking
- Friendly, sociable, and warm

CHALLENGES
- Strong reactions to anxieties
- Contrasting approaches to change
- Highly reactive in conflict

LOVING IN HARMONY

Even though these two gain so much from their differences, they have a fair amount of similarities. They are both sociable, kind, warm, and enjoy spending time with loved ones. They are charming, focused on the future, and usually enjoy quick-witted humor. Sixes are initially attracted to the way Sevens are so adventurous and spontaneous; it encourages them to be more free-spirited themselves. Sevens like how loyal, trustworthy, and lively Sixes are. This couple can be a fun-loving and charming pair!

CHALLENGES

The primary challenge for this couple is rooted in their contrasting natures: Sixes are serious and committed; Sevens value their freedom and autonomy highly and can almost veer toward noncommittal. This fuels Sixes' fear of being abandoned, causing them to worry, stress, and want more than Sevens are willing or inclined to give. If Sixes push too much, Sevens will feel claustrophobic and limited, which triggers their own fears and ignites their anxiety to run or flee.

CONFLICT RESOLUTION

Sixes need reassurance. Even if their fears seem irrational, it's important that Sevens ease their anxieties and not brush them off. In the moment, Sixes' feelings of fear of abandonment are all very real; Sevens can resolve their conflicts sooner if they understand that. Sixes will need to practice seeing the silver lining sometimes (the way Sevens do) and coming from a positive place. This will help both of them enjoy each other's company more.

TYPE SIX & TYPE EIGHT

STRENGTHS
- Protective over loved ones
- Committed and resilient
- Bond over the need for safety

CHALLENGES
- Intense skepticism
- Highly reactionary
- Overpowering emotions

LOVING IN HARMONY

This couple shares an understanding of trust and honesty, and a need to feel completely safe and comfortable with one another. They might even bond over how much they do not easily trust others. Both of them crave honesty and forthrightness, which they both naturally bring to the relationship. Sixes are usually attracted to how self-confident and loyal Eights can be, and Eights respect the commitment and devotion Sixes bring to the partnership. Together, they can slowly build an unbreakable bond with intense emotional depth.

CHALLENGES

This couple can be easily triggered by the other's emotional reactivity. Sixes might be intimidated at first by Eights' challenging and confrontational style, leading them to doubt their loyalty to themselves, the relationship, or both. Eights don't typically have much patience for Sixes' indecisive nature. Eights might see this as a challenge to empower their Six to become more assertive. When they search for solutions to problems, Eights and Sixes are usually too emotionally charged and can be susceptible to saying things that they don't mean out of anger.

CONFLICT RESOLUTION

It will benefit this couple to learn how to calm their emotions and reactions before approaching each other to resolve a conflict. They'll need to understand that their natural inclination when they are under stress will often be to accuse, confront, and counterattack. It's best if Sixes practice asserting themselves and their position. For Eights, it will be helpful if they listen more and start to work on softening their domineering inclinations that put Sixes into a state of fear.

TYPE SIX & TYPE NINE

STRENGTHS
- Understand each other's needs
- Committed to their relationships
- Value security and peace of mind

CHALLENGES
- Contrasting approaches to conflict
- Difficulty leaving toxic circumstances
- Overly dependent on what others think

LOVING IN HARMONY

Although these two Types embody opposing worldviews, they always find understanding and compassion for how the other operates. Their similarities include generosity, empathy, and being family- and friend-oriented. They both value and care deeply for their relationships. Sixes are generally attracted to how calm and easygoing Nines can be—they feel safe and comforted by their presence. Nines appreciate the support and warmth Sixes bring to the relationship. Through their strengths, Sixes and Nines can foster a stable and loving relationship.

CHALLENGES

It's their similarities that stress this relationship. They're both indecisive, afraid of ruffling feathers (they tend to avoid conflict), and quite unclear about how to communicate what they want and need. These stressors bring out Sixes' fear and Nines' stubborn behavior, especially when Sixes are trying to push or provoke them. This pair can often find themselves in a cycle of worst-case-scenario thinking that lands them both in stress-induced patterns of behavior.

CONFLICT RESOLUTION

In order to combat unhealthy patterns of stress and anxiety, Sixes need to practice cultivating an encouraging and optimistic approach with Nines. Finding a resolution is much easier for Nines when they are not being pressured. Sixes, on the other hand, need to let out steam and be heard—which Nines need to understand is Sixes' way of processing. If they give Sixes a bit of understanding and compassion, Nines can more easily find a resolution and move on.

TYPE SEVEN & TYPE SEVEN

STRENGTHS
- Stimulating conversation
- Outgoing, witty, and playful
- Resilient and perceptive

CHALLENGES
- Noncommittal and unreliable
- Impatient and self-serving
- Tendency to avoid deep emotions

LOVING IN HARMONY

It's going to be difficult to keep track of this couple. They thrive on fun, adventure, and new experiences. This is usually the spark that connects the two of them. Sevens are free-spirited and generally cheerful, and they have the energy to back it up. They can also be quite romantic and they love new beginnings. They'll never get bored of each other. With their ability to reframe difficult situations, they'll naturally focus on the good between them. This pairing can be quite popular and will probably radiate lots of positive vibes.

CHALLENGES

As with any double pairing, their challenges will be the catalyst for arguments. They can be escapists, not wanting to deal with their commitments and responsibilities. Problems arise when they want different things and don't quite know how to compromise for the other. They can be impulsive and insensitive, saying hurtful comments and causing several misunderstandings. When things become uncomfortable between them, they tend to distract themselves or escape, and put physical and emotional distance between each other.

CONFLICT RESOLUTION

One of the most important actions these two can take is to slow down. The only way to solve a problem is not to avoid it but to push through it. It's imperative for them to sit down and talk things out, truly listening to the other's complaints and concerns. They need to realize that when challenges arise, happiness and contentment will come to them if they stay committed to sticking things out.

TYPE SEVEN & TYPE EIGHT

STRENGTHS
- Assertive and confident
- Enjoy stimulating conversations
- Advocate for their happiness

CHALLENGES
- Tendency to overspend resources
- Impulsive and defiant
- Highly outspoken and blunt

LOVING IN HARMONY

This couple is bound and determined to not only enjoy themselves and their relationship, but also enjoy life as they see fit. They both value their freedom to do what they want, how they want. They admire this in each other and are often attracted to the energy and vitality they share. This couple has lots of pizzazz and gusto for life. Sevens are highly attracted to how Eights lead and protect; Eights can't get enough of Sevens' lighthearted and playful nature. As a pair, these two can be highly productive and unstoppable.

CHALLENGES

When it comes to what might create chaos for these two, well, it's going to stem from the fact that they can both be impulsive, unrestrained, and even out of control at times. They do not know when enough is enough, and that creates a chaotic and unruly lifestyle. Sevens often find Eights too controlling. Eights do not appreciate how flippant and unreliable Sevens can be. They will have a great deal of trouble keeping things from getting out of control.

CONFLICT RESOLUTION

Sevens and Eights need to learn how to de-escalate their arguments before they lead to insults and yelling. Sevens should learn to practice keeping their word and Eights should work on their tact and delivery. With as much energy as these two possess, it will be to their personal benefit and to the benefit of their relationship if they can take a few steps back during stressful moments of stress and conflict to realize that they're on the same team. Together they can find solutions if they keep a team player–like mentality.

TYPE SEVEN & TYPE NINE

STRENGTHS
- Able to forgive and forget
- Enjoy keeping things lighthearted
- Friendly and optimistic

CHALLENGES
- Neglect relationship issues
- Lack follow-through on promises
- Difficulty with introspection

LOVING IN HARMONY

These two are quite complementary to each other. They operate from different energetic levels: Sevens are typically high energy, and Nines are typically low energy; together, they can meet in the middle or keep each other balanced! Sevens are usually attracted to how adaptable and easygoing Nines are. Nines are intrigued by self-assertive and spontaneous Sevens. They're both optimistic, idealistic, and share a range of common interests.

CHALLENGES

This couple will find it hard to acknowledge that there are any challenges. They tend to be conflict-avoidant and don't know how to sit with uncomfortable emotions or situations. Nines usually withdraw and disconnect; Sevens keep themselves overly occupied so they don't have to deal with what's right in front of them. This can put quite a bit of distance between them and perhaps even cause a rift in their relationship.

CONFLICT RESOLUTION

Due to their avoidance of conflict, finding resolution will require that Sevens slow down and check in with Nines. They should be patient and listen intently, since it might take Nines a while to feel safe enough to freely speak their mind. Nines will have a natural tendency to let annoyances roll off their back. For them, they need to be aware of when they are feeling unsettled and to speak up when that occurs. When Sevens and Nines are more aware of and work through their difficulties, this effort will strengthen their bond.

TYPE EIGHT & TYPE EIGHT

STRENGTHS
- Highly supportive of each other
- Passionate and committed
- Direct and honest

CHALLENGES
- Insensitive and overly blunt
- Combative and reactive
- Controlling and overly self-protective

LOVING IN HARMONY

Two Eights in a loving and committed relationship form a partnership based on passion, power, and fierce energy. These two are brought together by their charismatic nature and directness. They enjoy being honest, up-front, and self-expressive with one another. They also find safety and trust in one another, which easily turns into a strong bond of commitment and determination. As they are body-oriented, they feel relaxed and at ease being themselves around each other. Overall, this combination of Types can make quite a strong and dynamic couple.

CHALLENGES

It won't be a surprise to this couple that they need to be very careful when it comes to their impulsivity and lack of vulnerability. They can be controlling and guarded when they feel stressed or fearful. They don't like to show weakness, so any sign of weakness in their partner can aggravate them. Under stress, they lack patience; arguments between them can often lead to feelings of anger or even rage.

CONFLICT RESOLUTION

The very first thing this couple will need to understand and accept about themselves and the other person is that they do not like being vulnerable. They are afraid to let their guard down because they're scared of being hurt. They do not want to be controlled or manipulated. Once these two can accept that, they can start to bring down the walls between them and build trust. Only then can they find true intimacy with their partners. They'll need to encourage this in each other and be open to feeling vulnerable time and time again.

TYPE EIGHT & TYPE NINE

STRENGTHS
- Romantic and loyal
- Possess great willpower
- Can endure great trials

CHALLENGES
- Lack of awareness
- Stubborn and hardheaded
- Controlling and passive-aggressive

LOVING IN HARMONY

At first glance, these two may come off as total opposites but, on the contrary, this dynamic very well may be why they fell in love. They're both down-to-earth, supportive, and loving—at least, once trust is fully established. Eights enjoy being around Nines' calming and accepting nature; Nines are usually attracted to how steady and strong Eights can be. This couple is highly instinctual; when they form a true bond, their love can be everlasting.

CHALLENGES

The passivity of Nines and the demanding nature of Eights can be quite challenging for these two and often becomes the point of contention between them. Nines have difficulty speaking up for themselves, a tendency that may be exacerbated by strong Eights who shut them down. Nines can often feel dominated by Eights' mere presence; Eights typically become frustrated by Nines' lack of initiative. Their strong-willed nature makes it difficult for this pair to meet in the middle.

CONFLICT RESOLUTION

Most often, especially with this couple, resolution can be found when they both relinquish their need for control. Control looks very different for each of them, however. Eights seek it through power, whereas Nines find it by being silently stubborn. If they want to find resolution and make their way back to each other, they'll need to practice letting go, being patient with the other's differences, and recognizing how their own behavior is affecting their relationship.

TYPE NINE & TYPE NINE

STRENGTHS
- Steady and peaceful
- Value harmony in their lives
- Accepting of things just as they are

CHALLENGES
- Stubborn and resistant to change
- Difficulty resolving conflict
- Procrastination and stagnation

LOVING IN HARMONY

This is a sweet, loving, and peaceful pairing. They share several of the same values, which creates a caring relationship based on compassion, acceptance, and an understanding that being content is paramount. These two love spending time together and often merge with what the other wants or needs. They are not overly affectionate in public, but within the privacy of their home, they are extremely thoughtful toward one another. Together, they find safety, love, and harmony within each other.

CHALLENGES

With the strong desire to keep things as harmonious as possible, these two will avoid conflict like the plague, especially if they don't have very strong Eight Wings. They do not want to be direct or disrupt the peace in their relationship, so they may hold onto feelings of anger, bitterness, and resentment toward each other. They are uncertain about how or when to let out their frustrations, which causes them anxiety and may lead to them shutting down altogether.

CONFLICT RESOLUTION

They need to learn how to identify what bothers them and what causes them pain, and how to communicate that to each other. Encouragement is key here! When it comes to resolving disputes, they will both be more willing to develop a plan of action if they know it will lead to a positive outcome. They should also check in with themselves daily as a form of self-love and as a way to strengthen the dynamic between them. Getting to know and understand how they feel internally is the start to them being able to express it to their partner.

6

Using the Enneagram to Improve Relationships at Work

TYPE ONE & TYPE ONE

STRENGTHS
- Organized and responsible
- Independent and self-starters
- Excellent follow-through

CHALLENGES
- Rigid thinking
- Perfectionistic
- Short-tempered

WORKING IN HARMONY

Ones have a very strong work ethic and hold themselves and others to very high standards. Therefore, two Ones in the workplace are likely to have a deep rapport with each other. They are both self-disciplined, and enjoy structure and routine. Once these two build trust through shared passions, they will feel a great deal of respect for each other. They can be counted on to find solutions to just about any problem in their field and will work together to make difficult decisions.

CHALLENGES

Ones tend to be perfectionists and can have very rigid thinking. They also have strong convictions about how things should be done and are hot-tempered. When working together, they will face obstacles head-on; if they don't agree on how to proceed, they will come to an impasse, both holding tightly to their opinions. Resentment and irritation can also build between them if they don't air their grievances.

CONFLICT RESOLUTION

Ones are open to dealing with conflict. In order for these two to get past their resentments, however, they need to acknowledge responsibility for their actions and be direct about why they are angry. They should also avoid criticizing or using harsh language with each other during conflict. It's important for them to stay open-minded to others' points of view, especially those they may disagree with.

TYPE ONE & TYPE TWO

STRENGTHS
- Reliable ethical standards
- Strong focus on customer service
- Strive to be of good use

CHALLENGES
- Find it difficult to indulge
- Always want to be right
- Can let resentment build

WORKING IN HARMONY

These two are both service-oriented individuals who enjoy feeling needed. They excel at helping others and understanding that sometimes you have to sacrifice a little to get the job done. They work well together when Twos prove themselves to be reliable and when Ones are willing to display compassion.

CHALLENGES

Twos frequently offer their advice, but when that advice is aimed directly at Ones, they hear it as criticism. Twos, who only "want to help," will feel rejected and hurt by Ones' reactions, which will only make matters worse. At work, if Twos become emotional, Ones remain rational and emotionally disconnected, offering no sympathy. Ultimately, Twos will feel that Ones don't appreciate them.

CONFLICT RESOLUTION

Ones need to understand that Twos are usually coming from a place of wanting to help, not criticize. Instead of responding negatively toward Twos, Ones can build rapport with them by showing their appreciation. Twos need to understand that Ones don't respond well to criticism; though Twos are only trying to help, they should ask if their help is wanted before proceeding.

TYPE ONE & TYPE THREE

STRENGTHS
- Self-disciplined and competent
- Responsible and polite
- Excel at creating efficiency

CHALLENGES
- Workaholics
- Perfectionists
- Fear of not being good enough

WORKING IN HARMONY

Ones and Threes value being productive and getting things done in an efficient and timely manner. They work well together on projects by combining Ones' attention to detail and Threes' optimistic spirit. They are both great at solving problems objectively and appreciate keeping emotions out of the mix. Ones admire the way Threes can take initiative; Threes know that they can count on Ones to do things the right way. Together, they make an effective and responsible team.

CHALLENGES

Ones don't react well to criticism, especially when someone is pointing out their flaws. Threes also don't like being perceived by others in a negative light. In a work environment, there's plenty of opportunity for both of them to call out the other when they think something could be better. Ones sometimes become inflexible if Threes try to challenge the way they are doing something. Threes may try to cut corners to get a job done, which can provoke Ones to stand on their moral high ground and demand doing things to their high standards.

CONFLICT RESOLUTION

Ones and Threes are both in the Competency Triad, which means when it comes to conflict resolution, they both approach issues emotionally detached and wanting to resolve things in a logical and systematic way. They will benefit by being honest and straightforward, and by actively listening to each other's point of view. If they have the same goal of wanting to quickly find a solution, they'll usually be able to work something out in a timely manner.

TYPE ONE & TYPE FOUR

STRENGTHS
- Blend of logic and intuition
- High ideals and ethical
- Strive toward excellence

CHALLENGES
- Controlling
- Defensive and sensitive to criticism
- Easily discouraged

WORKING IN HARMONY

Ones and Fours are typically focused on how to improve their environment along with themselves. In a work setting, this pair will usually be the first ones to notice how the atmosphere could be improved to be aesthetically appealing and more inviting for a better customer experience. Ones take notice of how creative and subjective Fours can be; Fours are usually inspired by how action-oriented Ones can be. Through effective communication, this pair can be highly complementary at work.

CHALLENGES

Ones can become agitated by Fours' emotionality. Ones work with a very focused mindset; Fours' moodiness will interfere with their objectives. Fours often view Ones as arrogant, stubborn, and unwilling to compromise or see other ways of doing something. They'll often get into arguments over how things should or shouldn't be done. Fours can become emotional; Ones usually refrain from outbursts. Ones can harbor resentment against Fours and perceive them as being too emotional and, therefore, "unprofessional."

CONFLICT RESOLUTION

Ones need to be able to hold space for Fours in order to find solutions at work. When Fours feel understood by Ones, they're more likely to want to find solutions. Fours need to practice steadying their emotions while at work if they want to be taken seriously by Ones. They both need to learn how to accept constructive criticism and not fly off the handle when their mistakes are pointed out.

TYPE ONE & TYPE FIVE

STRENGTHS
- Rational and objective
- Responsible and careful
- Great at focusing on the task at hand

CHALLENGES
- Critical and rigid
- Sarcastic and judgmental
- Superiority complex

WORKING IN HARMONY

Ones and Fives are often the intellectual ones at work. They bring logic and critical thinking to new heights, which often results in the creation of systems that improve the work experience for everyone. Ones do quite well with Fives in the workplace because Fives, like Ones, value integrity, grit, and good problem-solving skills. This pair is not only highly effective; when it comes to expertise, they both strive to know as much as they can in their respective fields.

CHALLENGES

Ones can be extremely idealistic. Sometimes, however, when they have an idea of how things should be, it can be quite difficult for them to let go if their plans don't work out. Fives, on the other hand, usually deal quite well with change and can find a way to adjust. Fives can be rigid when it comes to what is expected of them and become quite overwhelmed in high-stress situations. This is where Ones often excel—they can take the lead when more is being asked of them.

CONFLICT RESOLUTION

Ones and Fives are both in the Competency Triad, making them quite effective at resolving conflict in a fair, logical, and timely manner. Ones will need to practice letting go of the need to be right, and Fives will need to be less critical of Ones' performance. Fives can also practice expressing some emotion by encouraging Ones to be less critical of themselves, allowing Ones to be more effective.

TYPE ONE & TYPE SIX

STRENGTHS
- Loyal and committed to hard work
- Ability to persevere
- Strong sense of duty

CHALLENGES
- Procrastination
- Sensitive to criticism
- Take on too much responsibility

WORKING IN HARMONY

Ones and Sixes make a hardworking duo! They are not only committed to their responsibilities but they are also willing to help others with their workloads. They both have the energy and drive to sustain a productive work environment. Ones like working with Sixes; Sixes are dedicated to doing things right and they're usually good company too. Sixes feel supported when they're working alongside Ones. This pair is excellent at prioritizing and maintaining good, consistent work.

CHALLENGES

Ones tend to get overly critical, which can easily upset Sixes, especially if the criticism is delivered publicly. If they feel cornered, Sixes are likely to become reactive and combative with Ones. Sixes can become insecure and anxious about their work if they're not receiving enough positive feedback. Ones will likely become frustrated at this and distance themselves from them. Both of them will find it difficult to work together if they're unable to understand each other.

CONFLICT RESOLUTION

Ones and Sixes need to build trust in order to find solutions to their problems. Ones can do so by affirming Sixes' instincts when Sixes need a bit of guidance and support. Sixes can practice being reliable and offering their own form of support to show that they appreciate Ones. With a fair amount of patience and reassurance, this pair can settle tensions so they can find solutions sooner.

TYPE ONE & TYPE SEVEN

STRENGTHS
- Action-oriented
- Enjoy learning new things
- Work great independently

CHALLENGES
- Arrogant and impatient
- Justify all their actions
- Selfish and demanding

WORKING IN HARMONY

Ones and Sevens have a very different approach to how to get things done and how they want to work. However, these differences can be useful to both of them. Ones will usually want things done in an orderly fashion, whereas Sevens are more motivated by pleasure. If they combine their strengths, they're able to work together in a way that will maximize their goals. Ones also like to have fun, so when it comes to working with Sevens, they're able to get creative, play, and explore new ideas. Sevens are able to learn how to be more self-disciplined and efficient like Ones. Together, they complement each other.

CHALLENGES

If Ones become overly controlling and expect results that are unattainable, Sevens will likely become stressed and not want to be around Ones. They'll feel as if nothing will ever be good enough for them.

Ones can also become frustrated by Sevens' lack of focus and self-centeredness, with the result that they are even more critical and judgmental of Sevens. Ones will likely lose respect for Sevens, and Sevens will not understand why Ones are being so rigid and boring.

CONFLICT RESOLUTION

In order for this pairing to work well together, they both have to understand where the other one is coming from. Ones will have to practice being more open-minded to new experiences; they can build rapport with Sevens by asking for their input on projects and tasks. To help build trust with Ones, Sevens need to develop a stronger sense of responsibility and honor their commitments. These two can resolve conflict by respecting where the other person is coming from, even if it's contrary to what they themselves value.

TYPE ONE & TYPE EIGHT

STRENGTHS
- Practical and determined
- Value doing the right thing
- Self-reliant and purposeful

CHALLENGES
- Difficulty admitting fault
- Impatient and stubborn
- Always want to be in charge

WORKING IN HARMONY

Ones and Eights are inclined to take the initiative and therefore make great leaders. They were born to make decisions, even difficult and complicated decisions. Together, they usually get a lot accomplished and are often driven by their need to do good for others. They're both honest and hardworking. Ones are usually impressed by how passionate Eights can be, and Eights appreciate the way Ones are willing to sacrifice in order to get things done right. They make a magnetic and strong team.

CHALLENGES

Who's in charge? This will become an issue that these two confront often. Ones and Eights both want to take the lead and have no qualms about expressing how they believe things should be. If neither one of them lets the other take the reins, these two might become aggressive, combative, and rude. Eights will not care for the way Ones are often on their "high horse." Ones may feel attacked by how insensitive Eights can seem. This conflict may eventually devolve into arguing and perhaps even yelling.

CONFLICT RESOLUTION

For these two, it's a matter of relinquishing control and calming down before approaching each other. Eights, who have no issues with confrontations, usually gain energy from them. This will not benefit them in the workplace, however, so they'll need to practice steadying their emotionally reactive behaviors. Ones need to stop being overly rigid with how they think things should be and understand that Eights are usually after the same goal as they are. They both have strong convictions that will have to be talked out in an unemotional and friendly way if they want to work together effectively.

TYPE ONE & TYPE NINE

STRENGTHS
- Enjoy being of service to others
- Share fundamental values
- Great listeners and hospitable

CHALLENGES
- Procrastination and indecision
- Repressed anger
- A tendency to become stubborn

WORKING IN HARMONY

Ones and Nines both have great instincts when it comes to maintaining control in any given situation. They work well together because they enjoy working in a peaceful environment, eschew office drama, and value predictability. Ones like working alongside Nines because they're even-tempered and can be very calming to work with. Nines sometimes have difficulty making decisions and appreciate how Ones are great at showing them how to lead. They make a friendly and dependable team.

CHALLENGES

Ones can quickly overpower Nines by pushing them too hard. Nines need more time to think things through and process. In reaction, Ones become frustrated, impatient, and critical of Nines, who become stubborn and withdraw. Nines do not appreciate how Ones can make them feel inferior. This can turn into a silent standoff where neither one of them is willing to open up because they're both inwardly seething with anger at the other. Eventually, things will erupt and all the issues they've been holding in will spill out in a mean and possibly cruel way.

CONFLICT RESOLUTION

As it is peace and order these two are looking for in the workplace, they'll have to remember that the other wants the same thing. How they go about working with one another will take some patience and effective communication. Ones need to learn to read Nines' cues when they are becoming overwhelmed with their demands. Instead of telling Nines what to do, Ones should check in with Nines and solicit their opinion. Nines will need to stay present during conflict resolution in order to accomplish goals and be a team player.

TYPE TWO & TYPE TWO

STRENGTHS
- Attentive and empathetic
- Caring and understanding
- Helpful and adaptable

CHALLENGES
- Prideful and possessive
- Codependent
- Easily feel unappreciated

WORKING IN HARMONY

Twos in the workplace are ready to help and give assistance at a moment's notice. They're reliable and enjoy building personal connections—not just with each other but with everyone else they work with. They want to make sure they're being of service to others. They excel at customer service, creating a warm and friendly environment, and easily adapt to changes. Twos will often check in with each other to ensure the emotional well-being of their cohort. Together, they make a supportive and attentive team.

CHALLENGES

What usually causes tension between these two is a lack of awareness of how they feel and what they need. They can and will become so focused on everything else around them that they'll neglect themselves and their work. They might spend so much time helping others that they'll run behind on their own deadlines. They seek deep emotional connection; because of this, they may become overly competitive with each other over who is coming to them for help.

CONFLICT RESOLUTION

This pair needs to build healthy boundaries between each other and those in the office. They need to direct more of their energy inward as to not become overly focused on each other or others. They can encourage each other to stay focused on their own tasks, offer help only when they've finished their responsibilities first, and work independently of each other as much as possible.

TYPE TWO & TYPE THREE

STRENGTHS
- Great interpersonal skills
- Action-oriented and positive
- Energetic and friendly

CHALLENGES
- Need a lot of recognition
- Self-image more important than honesty
- Overly flattering

WORKING IN HARMONY

Twos and Threes typically get along great in the workplace. They're both lively and upbeat, with a surplus of positive energy to keep each other motivated. Threes are goal-oriented. Twos appreciate this about them, especially because it helps them to stay focused on the task at hand. Threes can "read a room" in order to know what is expected of them, which complements Twos' ability to immediately know what the room needs. Their friendly vibe and drive for success make them a great sales and marketing team!

CHALLENGES

Since these two are a bit image-conscious and tend to seek validation from outside sources, they can easily become competitive with each other. Jealously will likely come between them. When it's time to take credit for a project or a task, they both may seek the limelight and argue over who did what in order to be praised and admired for a job well done. On the other hand, if something goes wrong, they will likely dodge responsibility or even blame the other.

CONFLICT RESOLUTION

The key factors that allow Twos and Threes to work effectively together include being honest, staying authentic, and accepting constructive criticism with an open mind. They're both sensitive to criticism and will often avoid taking responsibility so as to not be seen in an unfavorable light. So, they both need to practice acknowledging their own flaws, taking ownership of them, and finding a way to work together that allows room for error. This strategy will also help them build trust between each other.

TYPE TWO & TYPE FOUR

STRENGTHS
- Supportive and kind
- Creative and intuitive
- Good listeners

CHALLENGES
- Sensitive to criticism
- Overly involved in the affairs of others
- Carry unnecessary guilt

WORKING IN HARMONY

Twos and Fours foster a workplace atmosphere of acceptance, warmth, and kindness. They enjoy deep conversations and typically do well on projects that spark their interest, which allows them to dive into their creativity and self-expression. Fours like working alongside Twos because they bring out their lighthearted side. Twos can be influenced by Fours' ability to be authentic and emotionally honest. They make a compassionate and knowledgeable team.

CHALLENGES

Working together for long periods of time brings out several stressors for these two. Fours can become very moody and dissatisfied with themselves. This can aggravate Twos, who usually want to work in a positive and uplifting environment. Twos may begin to see Fours as self-involved or even ungrateful. Fours will cringe at what comes across as inauthenticity when Twos excessively flatter someone. As they become increasingly bothered by each other, they will need to take some space and time to dispel any unpleasant feelings about the other so that they can work together again.

CONFLICT RESOLUTION

As both Twos and Fours are sensitive creatures, they need to be careful to modulate the energy they're displaying at work. Even though they try to hide their feelings, these Types are usually unable to suppress their true emotions. What helps these two work together most effectively is taking care of their own needs, and being supportive and helpful to each other in the process.

TYPE TWO & TYPE FIVE

STRENGTHS
- Able to balance emotions with logic
- Loyal and trustworthy
- Kind and thoughtful

CHALLENGES
- Difficulty asking for what they need
- Contrasting approach to emotions
- Become obsessive in their thinking

WORKING IN HARMONY

Although Twos and Fives are very unlike one another, their differences can create a great balance of critical thinking, personal connection, and loyalty to their responsibilities in the workplace. When they work alongside Fives, Twos become much more focused. In contrast, Fives become much more aware of others and how their behavior is affecting the work environment. When these two work on tasks and projects, they become highly competent and are able to produce excellent results. They make a helpful and skillful team.

CHALLENGES

Under stress, Twos tend to become needy and almost too dependent on Fives, which causes Fives to withdraw. As a result, Twos feel rejected and begin to see Fives as cold and callous. Fives don't necessarily care that this is happening, which only makes matters worse.

Fives work with usually just one objective—to focus on and complete their responsibilities. In contrast, Twos need more personal connections at work. This can create a cycle of negative stress that will likely end in both having angry outbursts.

CONFLICT RESOLUTION

For Twos and Fives, it's best if they start by understanding where the other is coming from. Twos need to realize that Fives require a great deal of autonomy, and they do not want to be expected to meet Twos' emotional needs. Fives can learn from Twos' compassionate and giving nature that they're looking for a bit of connection. It will benefit Fives to open up a little and learn how to politely express when they need space. Twos, of course, need to not take this personally and respect Fives' boundaries.

TYPE TWO & TYPE SIX

STRENGTHS
- Friendly and dutiful
- Make great team players
- Committed to their responsibilities

CHALLENGES
- Difficulty making decisions
- Issues with self-starting
- Procrastination

WORKING IN HARMONY

Twos and Sixes are extremely helpful and kind at work, and ready to get the job done, no matter how long it takes. They're committed to doing good work and making others happy in the process. They want to make sure things are done in a fair and optimal manner. Twos appreciate how meticulous Sixes are, whereas Sixes find Twos' positive nature calming and reassuring. They're both ready to serve the greater good and make a high-functioning, community-minded team.

CHALLENGES

Sixes usually err on the side of caution and can sometimes become skeptical about people's motives and intentions—so much, in fact, that it inhibits their ability to make decisions. Twos will eventually tire of their fearful and anxious energy. Both these Types are inclined to have anxious energy, and in stressful situations they typically feed off of each other's negative vibes. They will become increasingly reactive toward each other and completely lose focus on the task at hand. Sixes can become accusatory; Twos can become too overwhelmed to work alongside them.

CONFLICT RESOLUTION

In order to create an environment where these two can thrive and be effective, it will take some empathy on both their parts. Twos will need to understand that most of the pessimistic and anxious energy Sixes hold is coming from their need for security. Sixes can try to be more open about how they're feeling and accept some reassurance. This will create a safe space for both of them to see past their issues and focus on their work.

TYPE TWO & TYPE SEVEN

STRENGTHS
- Sociable and energetic
- Flexible and capable
- Optimistic and engaging

CHALLENGES
- Overly dramatic
- Unfocused and easily distracted
- Always want to be in charge

WORKING IN HARMONY

Twos and Sevens bring a positive and upbeat attitude to the office, and work best in that kind of environment. They tend to be the ones who volunteer to plan an office party or lead a team-building activity for everyone to come together and have some fun. Twos are usually motivated to work with Sevens because they admire Sevens' enthusiasm. Sevens do well working alongside Twos because of Twos' ability to be flexible. These two make the workplace a fun and happy place to come to every day.

CHALLENGES

Twos and Sevens find it a challenge to stay on task, get through difficult assignments, or maintain focus while working on projects they deem boring or daunting. Under stress or pressure, Twos can become domineering and may lash out at Sevens for being what they consider selfish and irresponsible. Sevens can regard Twos as intrusive and manipulative. Twos will feel unappreciated for their efforts. In contrast, Sevens will tire of having to constantly give them positive affirmations for the work they do.

CONFLICT RESOLUTION

Twos and Sevens should encourage each other to stay focused when deadlines are upon them or when they have committed themselves to a project. When conflict does arise during their time working together, they should use open and constructive communication immediately. Neither of these Types cares for conflict, but they need to come to the table with honesty and a willingness to acknowledge the negative feelings and situations that come up at work. Sevens need to resist the urge to brush off any negative emotions expressed by Twos, and Twos need to develop a stronger sense of their own independence.

TYPE TWO & TYPE EIGHT

STRENGTHS
- Strong-willed and determined
- Excellent social skills
- Responsible and pragmatic

CHALLENGES
- Easily angered and controlling
- Difficulty respecting boundaries
- Aggressive and forceful

WORKING IN HARMONY

Twos and Eights can have a great deal of influence on a work environment. Twos help Eights soften their approach; Eights show Twos how to protect themselves by creating healthy boundaries. Due to the fact that they are action-oriented, they typically work well on projects that require physical energy and that are aimed at helping others. They both want to see equality and fairness in the workplace. The charm of Twos combined with the magnetism of Eights makes them quite a powerful team.

CHALLENGES

During times of stress, Eights tend to become overbearing and domineering with Twos. As a result, Twos begin to feel uneasy or possibly even afraid. Eights don't tolerate signs of weakness or vulnerability in the workplace; Twos can trigger this intolerance by being overly emotional, dependent, and clingy. They may become hostile toward each other and even lose respect for one another if they do not resolve their issues in a timely manner.

CONFLICT RESOLUTION

It's crucial that this pair remains calm and collected when trying to resolve conflict. Eights need to work on calming down their reactivity toward Twos. This allows Twos to feel safe and able to speak up for themselves. As soon as Twos find a way to express their concerns or feelings in a straightforward and guileless manner, Eights will take them seriously and become more open to trusting them.

TYPE TWO & TYPE NINE

STRENGTHS
- Positive outlook
- Hospitable and friendly
- Accommodating and understanding

CHALLENGES
- Avoidant tendencies
- Difficulty saying no
- Reluctant to speak up for themselves

WORKING IN HARMONY

Twos and Nines bring a lot of positive energy to the workplace. They have a mutual understanding of each other's need for kindness, respect, and support. They are both usually happy and enjoy working in an orderly and hospitable environment. Twos and Nines are both easy to get along with, which is important for their relationships with coworkers. Twos usually find Nines' calming nature to be helpful during stressful work situations. Nines enjoy working with Twos because of their upbeat and fun nature. These two make a responsive and considerate team.

CHALLENGES

Though neither of these two relish conflict, they may find themselves disagreeing over prioritization of projects or deadlines. Twos work well when they fully understand what is expected of them. They can become quite persistent about getting things done in the way they see fit. Nines may perceive Twos' tenacity as controlling or even domineering at times; they do not respond well to Twos' pressure and will often find themselves avoiding them. Twos may become increasingly frustrated with Nines for being difficult and stubborn.

CONFLICT RESOLUTION

Even though these two have a great deal of empathy, they can find it difficult at work to operate from an emotional place because of all the other factors at play. However, when it comes to working well together and getting past issues that inhibit them, it's important that they air out their differences right away. They should avoid putting off even the slightest offense, as it can quickly grow into a much larger problem.

TYPE THREE & TYPE THREE

STRENGTHS
- Value accomplishment
- Goal-oriented
- Self-reliant and highly competent

CHALLENGES
- Overly competitive
- Workaholics
- Tendency to be opportunistic

WORKING IN HARMONY

When Threes work together, they will likely set some lofty goals for themselves and their coworkers. They thrive as a team because they are both hardworking and value achievement, prestige, and, most of all, success! They encourage each other to keep going when the going gets tough and will often act as "cheerleaders" for each other for moral support. They both have their eyes on the prize and will stop at nothing to finish projects with flying colors. They make an energetic and winning team.

CHALLENGES

What usually throws these two a curveball in their otherwise efficient dynamic is their competitiveness. They find it difficult to share credit on projects, and may even cheat or lie to ensure that they are the ones who come out on top to receive the glory. Their egotistical tendencies have the potential to create jealousy. If one is up for a promotion, the other may get envious and plot against them. These are examples of extreme behavior, but when the stakes are high, Threes do have it in them to be ruthless.

CONFLICT RESOLUTION

Threes will need to work on building trust and respect for each other in order for them to maintain a healthy working relationship. They can do so by motivating each other and showing their support for the other on their wins, no matter how big or small. They should make it a point to share their happiness when they've reached one of their goals. Or, they can open up and let each other know that they are there for them if they ever need a helping hand.

TYPE THREE & TYPE FOUR

STRENGTHS
- Innovative
- Creative problem-solvers
- Ambitious and authentic

CHALLENGES
- Tendency to seek approval
- Aloof and conceited
- Impatient and self-involved

WORKING IN HARMONY

Threes and Fours function well in the workplace as long as they're able to express themselves and feel accepted by each other. They complement each other because they play off of each other's strengths. Fours can teach Threes how to determine what they really want, instead of what everyone expects of them. Threes can show Fours how to achieve goals that they consider they are not capable or worthy of. Together, these two can make an inspiring team.

CHALLENGES

Achievement and success, which seems to come more easily to Threes, can upset Fours. This can often create jealousy in Fours, who may feel rejected and even inherently flawed. Fours want to be recognized at work for their unique ideas and creativity. Threes often see Fours as impractical and overly emotional. Fours can easily be turned off by what they perceive as Threes' phoniness or need for constant validation.

CONFLICT RESOLUTION

Threes need to learn how to be patient with Fours' tendency to do only what is expected of them at work. They need to become more open-minded and respect that Fours have a great creative vision that they should be allowed to express. Fours can get more accomplished at work if they steady their emotions and practice taking cues from Threes to get things done even if they don't feel like it. Both of them can learn a great deal from each other about how to effectively and emotionally tune in to themselves at work.

TYPE THREE & TYPE FIVE

STRENGTHS
- Logical and objective
- Independent workers
- Self-reliant and reliable

CHALLENGES
- Sensitive to criticism
- Overly competitive
- Obsessed with details

WORKING IN HARMONY

Threes and Fives are extremely logical and objective in the workplace. They both work well independently. As much as Fives enjoy their autonomy, they're most suited to team up with Threes to work on a project. Fives respect their self-confidence and competence. Threes can acknowledge Fives' insight and expertise; it also motivates them to know that their teamwork has brought them that much closer to reaching their goals. These two combine ambition with mastery, making themselves a highly effective team.

CHALLENGES

Threes can be a bit too enthusiastic and energetic for Fives. Fives often need time alone if they are working on a project. Threes might read this as Fives being disengaged and uninterested. If Threes try to cut corners on a project or assignment, Fives will likely call them out on it and may even become angry at their lack of ethics. Threes can sometimes make decisions too quickly, which leads them to make less-than-ideal choices. Though that situation is more likely to happen during times of high stress, Fives will nevertheless get angry at what they perceive as Threes' incompetence.

CONFLICT RESOLUTION

As these two are both in the Competency Triad, it is best that they take an objective and logical point of view when solving problems or dealing with their own personal misgivings at work. Both want to resolve problems quickly, but it's imperative that they take the time to address any concerns the other might have.

TYPE THREE & TYPE SIX

STRENGTHS
- Productive and goal-oriented
- Practical and responsible
- Respectable and service-oriented

CHALLENGES
- Tendencies toward workaholism
- Need a lot of external reassurance
- Put themselves under a lot of pressure

WORKING IN HARMONY

At work, Threes and Sixes are cooperative and generally make great team players. Sixes are loyal and kind, and are therefore a supportive teammate for Threes. Sixes respect and admire how self-confident and service-oriented Threes can be. Sixes feel that they can rely on Threes to work hard, as they do. Both of them are effective networkers and community builders. They are both personable and diplomatic when it comes to work-related issues, making them an energetic and loyal team.

CHALLENGES

Threes are self-starters who are used to taking the lead. When they work alongside Sixes, Threes might get impatient with their indecision and anxious energy. Threes are the kind of person to get things done, no matter what. They will do whatever it takes and this will cause Sixes to question their loyalty—not just to them, but to whatever task they are assigned to. Sixes err on the side of caution and don't necessarily like breaking the rules. This will irritate Threes and will eventually cause both of them to dislike the other.

CONFLICT RESOLUTION

Threes will need to be much more patient with Sixes, who are only trying to do things as they were told to be done. Brave Sixes may not care too much, if at all, about breaking rules, but, in general, they don't want to lose the support of those in authority. Sixes should practice directly communicating their point of view to Threes. They can both reach common ground if they listen to where the other is coming from.

TYPE THREE & TYPE SEVEN

STRENGTHS
- Energetic go-getters
- Self-motivated
- Uplifting and encouraging

CHALLENGES
- Not the greatest listeners
- Tendency to take too many risks
- Overly indulgent and self-absorbed

WORKING IN HARMONY

Threes and Sevens at work are highly self-motivated and ready to take on most assignments. They both are typically multitalented with lots of drive and charisma. Threes can appreciate how experienced Sevens are. They love working with them because they usually share the same amount of enthusiasm. Sevens are thrilled to work alongside Threes because of the positive thinking and confidence they bring to their work. These two make a self-assertive and high-energy team.

CHALLENGES

Problems arise when Sevens perceive that Threes take their responsibilities too seriously. Threes want outside validation for their hard work. Recognition isn't a priority for Sevens; they may see Threes as superficial and obsessed with achievement. Sevens can be hard workers but they also value having fun and doing things that bring them pleasure. If these two lack a common goal, working together will be highly problematic.

CONFLICT RESOLUTION

Threes and Sevens typically don't have major problems working together; when they do, they can be resolved fairly easily. Threes can practice being honest and open about their motives right from the start when they work on projects with Sevens. Sevens need to remember to be gentle and kind when they give feedback to Threes. Together, they can build rapport based on their similarities, like valuing their independence and pursuing projects they both find interesting.

TYPE THREE & TYPE EIGHT

STRENGTHS
- Fierce and passionate
- Great leadership skills
- Entrepreneurial

CHALLENGES
- Tendency to overwork themselves
- Often argue over control
- Can want too much power

WORKING IN HARMONY

Threes and Eights in the workplace are great leaders and incredibly hard workers. They're both ambitious, highly competent, and enjoy taking on challenges. Threes and Eights want to get the job done well and efficiently—it's something they admire in each other. Threes can rely on Eights for their strength and determination; Eights appreciate how driven and confident Threes can be. They make quite an accomplished team.

CHALLENGES

Conflict between these two usually stems from control issues. Since they both make great leaders, there will be power trips between these two, especially during stressful situations. Eights can be controlling and do not like being told what to do; Threes are impatient and don't want to have to explain themselves to Eights. This dynamic inevitably leads to a struggle for control between the two of them. During arguments, they can become domineering and manipulative.

CONFLICT RESOLUTION

Trust and honesty are significant pillars to any healthy work relationship. For these two, they're absolutely essential. Threes will need to practice being honest and straightforward with Eights in order to gain their trust and respect. It's crucial for Eights to let down their guard when trying to build a rapport with Threes. By being supportive and encouraging, they're more likely to gain Threes' trust. Showing a little vulnerability is essential for both of them.

TYPE THREE & TYPE NINE

STRENGTHS
- Supportive and encouraging
- Diplomatic and likable
- Productive and optimistic

CHALLENGES
- Stubborn standoffs
- Can overcommit
- People-pleasing

WORKING IN HARMONY

Threes and Nines at work make a generally positive and productive team. They both can be incredibly idealistic and will want to make sure things are done in a particular fashion. They are pretty adaptable and supportive of each other. Threes usually have a great deal of energy, so Nines appreciate the unexpected boost they get when they're around them. Threes like working with Nines due to their humble nature. They make a committed and pleasant team.

CHALLENGES

Problems arise in this pair when Threes become overly demanding. Threes tend to get frustrated and angry if they see Nines procrastinate or lose focus on the job, behavior that can happen when Nines work under a lot of pressure. These two have a very different reaction when under stress. Threes bring more drive and determination to their work; Nines tend to disassociate themselves from the chaos. They may even abandon Threes altogether in order to complete assignments on their own. Threes then begin to lose respect for Nines and ultimately the trust between them is broken.

CONFLICT RESOLUTION

Threes need to practice encouraging and supporting Nines, which will help Nines reduce their tendency to procrastinate in reaction to stress. Any other response will only cause them to retreat more. Nines, on the other hand, should work on developing healthier coping mechanisms when stressful situations arise. They also need to practice being open and honest with Threes when they begin to feel pressured. Frank communication between these two should be done calmly and with positive reinforcements for both of them.

TYPE FOUR & TYPE FOUR

STRENGTHS
- Value authenticity
- Compassionate and kind
- Creative and wise

CHALLENGES
- Temperamental
- Highly reactive in conflict
- Self-absorbed and aloof

WORKING IN HARMONY

Fours in the workplace work well together. They have an immediate understanding of where the other is coming from. In addition, their inclination toward empathy helps on those days when their colleague is not feeling their best. Fours are passionate at work if they enjoy what they're doing and are able to express themselves. They're very understanding and patient when trying to solve difficult issues. They make a soulful and creative team.

CHALLENGES

These two can fall into comparison and jealousy traps. Since they are both striving to create and maintain their own unique identities, if one of them receives more acknowledgment about their style or skills, the other can feel jealous. This can translate into them feeling unworthy and may even lead to emotional outbursts verging on self-pity. Fours are quite sensitive and don't do well with criticism; it can make them feel misunderstood and isolated.

CONFLICT RESOLUTION

When two Fours deal with conflict in the workplace, it's best if they take turns listening to each other's point of view as well as feelings. Once both Fours have shared their perspectives, they can move on to finding a positive way to resolve conflict. If they try to avoid this emotional release, their problems will linger, which could prevent them from truly moving on.

TYPE FOUR & TYPE FIVE

STRENGTHS
- Strong, curious minds
- Introspective and open-minded
- Contemplative and inventive

CHALLENGES
- Sensitive to criticism
- Feel like outsiders
- Disengaged from reality

WORKING IN HARMONY

Fours and Fives are incredibly deep thinkers. They both crave knowledge and want to understand how and why things work. They function best in an environment where they can learn something new every day. Fours enjoy working with Fives because of their inquisitive minds; Fives enjoy Fours' creativity. They both relish discussing at length the projects they're passionate about. Together, they make a quirky and insightful team.

CHALLENGES

Fours and Fives have a very different emotional approach and process feelings very differently from each other, which can make it difficult for these two to effectively work together. Fours' natural inclination is to build an emotional connection with their coworkers. In contrast, Fives could feel put off by this or find Fours' need for intimacy intrusive. Fives may think that Fours are invading their privacy and acting inappropriately, especially in a work environment. Fours, on the other hand, may feel as though Fives are extremely detached and unapproachable.

CONFLICT RESOLUTION

Fours need to understand that Fives are not as emotionally available as they are. Fives need plenty of space and privacy to think and feel secure. Fours understand boundaries, so it's important for Fives to let Fours know what they need. A simple warning, such as, "I need to be left alone right now; it's nothing personal," will immediately let Fours know to step back until Fives come forward. Fours also need to be more aware of how their emotional states are affecting others in a work environment and adjust them accordingly.

TYPE FOUR & TYPE SIX

STRENGTHS
- Vivid imaginations
- Healthy dose of skepticism
- Supportive and reassuring

CHALLENGES
- Rebellious and oppositional
- Inferiority complex
- Tendency toward insecurity

WORKING IN HARMONY

Fours and Sixes in the workplace will have an easy time getting along. They're both sensitive, friendly, and generous. Fours have a great time working with Sixes, thanks to their quick wit and supportive nature. Sixes feel understood around Fours; they appreciate how reassuring and accepting they are. They both can be quite analytical and may even search for deeper answers on work-related topics. For example, before proceeding on projects, they'll both want to do the appropriate research in order to be thorough. Together, they make an empathetic and intuitive team.

CHALLENGES

When these two are under a great deal of stress at work, their insecurities and moodiness can emerge to challenge them both. Fours and Sixes tend to become codependent on the other, either for emotional support or decision-making. Both Fours and Sixes can feel insecure and doubt their abilities. As empathetic as they both are, they might become highly reactive toward each other. Sixes may feel as though they can't trust Fours; Fours may become tired of Sixes' accusatory behavior.

CONFLICT RESOLUTION

Because they sit in the Reactive Triad, Fours and Sixes can become overly emotional; during conflict, their feelings intensify. They need to find a way to steady their emotions and slow down their responsiveness, like taking deep breaths before approaching the other. And, because they both know how easily they can get flustered, they should refrain from using accusatory, judgmental language when speaking to each other.

TYPE FOUR & TYPE SEVEN

STRENGTHS
- Curious and excitable
- Value having unique experiences
- Enjoy interesting conversations

CHALLENGES
- Overly self-involved
- Impulsive and impatient
- Easily become sidetracked

WORKING IN HARMONY

Even though Fours and Sevens are quite different from each other, they find it interesting to work together. They quickly realize their coworkers' strengths and become quite effective together. Fours appreciate how curious and experimental Sevens can be. Sevens are able to bring out Fours' action-oriented qualities so they can be more productive. These two make a great complementary team.

CHALLENGES

Sevens' tendency to pursue pleasurable experiences over fulfilling their work commitments (like meeting a deadline or finishing a presentation) can be a problem for Fours, who feel that Sevens abandoned them in favor of following their own selfish pursuits. Sevens can feel constrained by Fours' intensity, need for deep conversation, and frequent mood swings. Both can be self-involved and unwilling to see the other's perspective, which can lead to childish arguments.

CONFLICT RESOLUTION

Fours need to practice being patient with Sevens and ignore their inclination to reframe everything into a positive (which Sevens do as a way to move on from negative or unpleasant situations). Fours feel comfortable experiencing moody and dark emotions, whereas Sevens try to escape them. Fours need to allow Sevens to keep their autonomy; Sevens can gain a different perspective if they're open to exploring deeper emotions.

TYPE FOUR & TYPE EIGHT

STRENGTHS
- Value honesty and authenticity
- Highly expressive
- Strong convictions

CHALLENGES
- Controlling and impulsive
- Combative and oppositional
- Domineering and volatile

WORKING IN HARMONY

Fours and Eights work well together and complement each other's strengths. Eights have a lot of respect for how Fours always seek the truth in people and in situations. Fours draw from Eights' powerful energy and vitality—it helps Fours resist their inclination to withdraw. They are both attracted to projects that make them feel alive and keep them on their toes. They make a complex yet committed team.

CHALLENGES

Fours are sensitive souls and, unfortunately, Eights may see this as a sign of weakness. In the workplace, Eights are typically so focused on what needs to get done that they spend most of their time in action mode, an approach that is entirely different from that of Fours. If they sense that Fours' emotional mood swings are slowing them down, Eights will call them out on it and may even get angry enough to start yelling at them. Fours can get emotionally volatile; unless the situation is controlled, it will become increasingly dramatic.

CONFLICT RESOLUTION

Since these two can be intense, they need to remind themselves to calm down before trying to problem-solve. They should check in with each other every once in a while to see if there is anything, either personal or professional, that needs to be resolved. Through every conflict they resolve together, they'll become increasingly more trusting of one another.

TYPE FOUR & TYPE NINE

STRENGTHS
- Highly creative
- Empathetic and understanding
- Idealistic and intuitive

CHALLENGES
- Stubborn and controlling
- Withdrawn and tense
- Hypersensitive

WORKING IN HARMONY

Fours and Nines are drawn to creativity and activities that don't require a great deal of energy. They're both highly intuitive, which can be useful when it comes to resolving disputes through mediation and assessing the needs of different departments. Fours enjoy working with Nines because they are usually nonjudgmental; they won't berate them if they make a mistake. Nines enjoy how special Fours make them feel. They both want connection and understanding, making this a very empathetic team.

CHALLENGES

Under strain, Fours can become highly critical and demanding. They may push Nines so much that Nines will become indifferent to Fours' needs and withdraw altogether. Fours suspect that Nine's judgmental behavior indicates that they are not owning up to their responsibilities. If conflict escalates to an argument, these two can feel disillusioned with each other, leaving them wondering what happened to the trust and understanding they once had.

CONFLICT RESOLUTION

The good news is that even in stressful situations, these two can quickly find solutions. Nines tend to avoid conflict, but with the help of very empathetic Fours, they will feel more comfortable expressing their opinions. Fours will also be able to voice their opinions; together, they can find a compromise in any conflict. They may also find it useful to give each other space and time to thoroughly think through decisions.

TYPE FIVE & TYPE FIVE

STRENGTHS
- Trustworthy and responsible
- Objective and logical
- Considerate and respectful of boundaries

CHALLENGES
- Skeptical and suspicious
- Seemingly arrogant
- Overintellectualize

WORKING IN HARMONY

Fives at work usually get along well. Because they're not very emotional, they stick to discussing work or common interests. They don't overshare and appreciate how the other respects their privacy. They do well at theorizing and researching together, and are usually fact-oriented. Although they prefer to work independently, they also work well as a unit because these two respect boundaries and don't take them personally. They make an intellectual and visionary team.

CHALLENGES

Poor communication and maybe even a bit of detachment from the working relationship can often lead to problems between Fives. They may feel inadequate or even incompetent if they sense they've been left out of the loop on projects or ideas. If working independently from each other, this situation might not cause much of an issue. However, if they are working together on an assignment, this rift could result in decreased productivity.

CONFLICT RESOLUTION

Fives are not very emotional and would prefer to solve problems in an objective and logical way. They both want to resolve issues quickly and will have their own ideas on how to get there. It's important for them to communicate when working together and to keep an open mind when it comes to listening to each other's solutions. A little encouragement or interest in the other's thoughts will help as well.

TYPE FIVE & TYPE SIX

STRENGTHS
- Curious and contemplative
- Great during a crisis
- Dependable and loyal

CHALLENGES
- Guarded and overly cautious
- Tendency to lack initiative
- Cynical and pessimistic

WORKING IN HARMONY

Fives and Sixes are both in the Head Center (also known as the Thinking Center), making them highly competent at work, especially when it comes to research and problem-solving. They love learning new things and respect each other's privacy, which is usually important for both of them. Fives' logical and analytical brain dovetails nicely with Sixes' quick-witted and engaging energy. They make an inquisitive and loyal team.

CHALLENGES

Fives often find Sixes difficult to work with because of their anxious mind and their constant need for reassurance. This situation can be exacerbated by Fives' habit of withdrawing into their head, which can trigger Sixes' fears that they did something wrong, especially if Sixes report to Fives. Uncertain of where they stand, Sixes will need to be reassured that everything is fine in order for them to continue their work. Fives may grow tired of and even angry about having to show Sixes how and what to do, which will likely cause Sixes to become highly reactionary.

CONFLICT RESOLUTION

Fives need to practice being thoughtful and checking in with Sixes, which will help to build trust between them. Sixes will appreciate this, but they would do well to keep in mind that Fives take much longer to absorb and process information. If a conflict should arise, Sixes need to learn how to remain calm and express themselves in a professional and nonreactionary way. These two have the potential to build trust with one another over time.

TYPE FIVE & TYPE SEVEN

STRENGTHS
- Curious and quick-witted
- Independent
- Highly productive

CHALLENGES
- Have restless energy
- Avoid commitments
- Stay in their imagination too long

WORKING IN HARMONY

Fives and Sevens make a great team that prefers to work on interesting and exploratory projects. They both enjoy learning new skills: Fives are apt to want to master their skill set, whereas Sevens are inclined to want to study a variety of topics. However, with a little encouragement from Fives, Sevens can learn to focus on one area. They both enjoy acquiring information and experimenting with new ideas. Together, they make a wise and experienced team.

CHALLENGES

Fives and Sevens, who are both in the Thinking Triad, are inclined to carry nervous energy. Fives can easily become frustrated with Sevens' restless energy and inclination to shirk their responsibilities. They may even feel sometimes as though they are having to "babysit" them. Sevens, sensing that they are a nuisance to Fives, may become anxious and want to flee the situation. They could easily overwhelm each other in a high-stress environment.

CONFLICT RESOLUTION

Instead of rejecting or being suspicious of it, Fives can acquire some of the positivity that Sevens bring to the table; this way, they're more likely to build rapport with them. Sevens need to learn how to concisely communicate their thoughts and ideas. These two can work well together if they both respect each other's desire for autonomy. Sevens can encourage Fives to go after opportunities, and Fives can help Sevens ground their ideas so they can be implemented.

TYPE FIVE & TYPE EIGHT

STRENGTHS
- Insightful and wise
- Respect each other's freedom
- Self-reliant and dependable

CHALLENGES
- Always need to be right
- Impatient with incompetence
- Overanalyze situations

WORKING IN HARMONY

Fives and Eights are confident and fair, and work well independently. They are both very observant, wise, and usually quite experienced in their field. Fives enjoy working with Eights for their strength, self-assertiveness, and ability to take charge. This helps Fives, who are less inclined to take action. Eights admire how focused and knowledgeable Fives can be. They make an insightful and highly functional team.

CHALLENGES

Fives and Eights are not very good at communicating. Eights come from an instinctual and gut-level place, and tend to move right into the action without much thought. Fives, on the other hand, are inclined to analyze a problem for hours. These different approaches can create several problems: Fives avoid approaching Eights because they feel intimated and don't like confrontation; Eights might see Fives' reserved nature as a threat and may suspect that Fives are hiding something.

CONFLICT RESOLUTION

They both need to work on improving their communication skills. Fives will need to develop a stronger sense of themselves and hold their ground when they are speaking to Eights. This benefits Fives and also earns the respect of Eights, who appreciate people who are honest and straightforward. Eights need to be more aware of how their energy affects Fives and cultivate a calmer presence to make it easier for Fives to approach them.

TYPE FIVE & TYPE NINE

STRENGTHS

- Undemanding and respectful
- Logical and open-minded
- Intellectual and dependable

CHALLENGES

- Conflict-avoidant
- Slow to initiate and take action
- Quickly withdraw when overwhelmed

WORKING IN HARMONY

Fives and Nines bring calm reliability to the workplace. They're both dependable and kind, and respect each other's need for space. Nines' accepting and relaxed nature makes it easy for Fives to work well alongside them. Nines want to work with Fives because of Fives' disarming demeanor and ability to engage in fascinating conversations. They are a thoughtful and stable team.

CHALLENGES

Fives and Nines are both conflict-avoidant, which means they are not going to have many disagreements (at least publicly). What will commonly happen is that these two will avoid communicating altogether if they are assigned to work together. They can both be slow to take action and leave tasks to the last minute. Fives can become impatient with Nines' indecision, and Nines will end up doing things themselves if Fives withdraw.

CONFLICT RESOLUTION

As coworkers, Fives and Nines need to build a rapport in order to stay present and connected. Fives should encourage Nines to make decisions by asking them thought-provoking questions that get to the heart of the matter; Nines appreciate being asked for their opinion. Fives are patient, so they can give Nines space and time to think, as long as the gesture is reciprocated. Nines should also be aware that Fives need their space, which Fives should communicate to them.

TYPE SIX & TYPE SIX

STRENGTHS
- Honest and fair
- Analytical and imaginative
- Helpful and friendly

CHALLENGES
- Anxious and worrisome
- Pessimistic and inflexible
- Highly reactive

WORKING IN HARMONY

Sixes are inherently hardworking individuals. They are typically committed to their responsibilities and their role in the workplace. They value being in good standing with those in authority and will often sacrifice their time and energy for the greater good. The abundance of strengths that Sixes bring to work include good organization, support of others, and dedication to the cause. They appreciate working alongside each other because they know they can depend on the other to always come through for them. They are a loyal and reliable team.

CHALLENGES

Sixes carry a lot of anxious energy. They are also inclined to be mistrustful and have a great deal of self-doubt. This can prove to be difficult when working together—they both need and want reassurance from one another. If they haven't built trust, they won't find what they're looking for. If there is ever a mistake that happens or uncertainty on how to proceed on an assignment, stress levels will rise—making them highly reactionary and defensive. With so much confusion going on in their minds, these two may begin to panic.

CONFLICT RESOLUTION

If they want a strong working relationship, Sixes need to build trust with each other from the moment they meet. This will help them work together in harmony and motivate them to help each other when either of them is overwhelmed or when tensions rise. They can start by encouraging each other to feel more confident in the work they produce and the decisions they make. They can also help each other to stay on the positive side of work situations.

TYPE SIX & TYPE SEVEN

STRENGTHS
- Intellectual
- Great at brainstorming solutions
- Think quickly on their feet

CHALLENGES
- Tendency to overreact
- Procrastinate
- Anxious and restless

WORKING IN HARMONY

Sixes and Sevens make a complementary team in the workplace. Sixes are loyal, trustworthy, and quite dutiful, characteristics that can be beneficial to Sevens. They're both friendly and mentally sharp. Sevens might be able to encourage Sixes to take more risks and to see the big picture. Sixes and Sevens can see the silver lining when things don't go the way they had anticipated. Together, they are a careful and optimistic team.

CHALLENGES

Sixes might find it difficult to work alongside Sevens when they are working on a project that requires dedication and focus—skills that don't come naturally to Sevens. Sevens may feel that their positive energy is being stifled by Sixes' constant rumination over what might go wrong. As both these Types are in the Head Center or Thinking Center, they have a tendency to become anxious, which will show up in contrasting ways: Sixes put their energy into working on the task at hand until it's complete, whereas Sevens want to move on to something else that is less difficult or boring.

CONFLICT RESOLUTION

Sevens can learn quite a bit about commitment and hard work from Sixes. If they follow through and stay on task, as Sixes often do, Sevens will be able to complete tasks more quickly and move on to other things. Sixes need to learn how to lighten up during times of stress; they can learn a lot from Sevens in this area. Sevens are able to see the light at the end of the tunnel and can help Sixes see it too, if they're willing.

TYPE SIX & TYPE EIGHT

STRENGTHS
- Trustworthy and dependable
- Action-oriented
- Supportive and committed

CHALLENGES
- Don't handle stress well
- Skeptical and testy
- Likely to become defensive

WORKING IN HARMONY

Sixes and Eights are both committed to being honest. They are hard workers who can be trusted with highly important work. They do extraordinarily well together if they have to persevere through challenging situations. They are the ones who will stick with it until the job is done. Sixes appreciate Eights' loyalty; they know they can depend on Eights, which means a lot to Sixes. Eights appreciate Sixes' supportive and thoughtful nature. They make a conscientious and steadfast team.

CHALLENGES

Problems arise when Sixes see how aggressive and challenging Eights can be. They don't appreciate the way Eights talk down to them and may retaliate against them or become highly reactionary. Sixes can grow fearful of Eights and even feel bullied by them. In fact, Sixes can be overly fearful in general, which will come off as a sign of weakness to Eights, who get so annoyed with Sixes' lack of self-confidence that they may not want to work with them at all.

CONFLICT RESOLUTION

Sixes and Eights need to learn how to both slow down their reactivity and practice communicating more effectively. The best way to do this is for Sixes to develop a greater sense of self so that they are able to hold their ground around Eights. Eights need to approach Sixes in a calm and mild manner. These two can work well together as long as they remind themselves that respecting one another is key.

TYPE SIX & TYPE NINE

STRENGTHS
- Supportive
- Cooperative and kind
- Accepting and reassuring

CHALLENGES
- Lack of self-confidence
- Battle with indecision
- Self-doubting

WORKING IN HARMONY

Sixes and Nines in a work environment want to create routine, order, and predictability. They encourage each other and give the other person the ability to be themselves. Sixes are happy working with Nines because their anxieties are calmed by Nines' peaceful demeanor. Nines appreciate Sixes for their knowledge and steadiness. Together they make a caring and stable team.

CHALLENGES

Sixes and Nines are likely to struggle with communicating about problems they encounter. They both want to avoid conflict and can stonewall each other as a way to avoid it. Sixes don't want to make waves, but will eventually become unnerved by how complacent and stubborn Nines can be. Nines prefer to think positively and will not appreciate how negative and pessimistic Sixes can be. Both will avoid speaking up about problems and tend to become passive-aggressive toward one another.

CONFLICT RESOLUTION

Both of them will need to develop a way to bring issues to the table without feeling overwhelmed with all the possible outcomes. They don't like conflict but will need to practice being candid, honest, and clear about what they are thinking. They both want peace, so Sixes should learn how to encourage Nines to share their opinions and ideas. Nines should practice developing their self-confidence and voicing their thoughts and concerns.

TYPE SEVEN & TYPE SEVEN

STRENGTHS
- Highly productive
- Sociable and multitalented
- Self-confident and accomplished

CHALLENGES
- Self-involved
- Become bored easily
- Scattered and unfocused

WORKING IN HARMONY

Sevens bring a positive and uplifting energy to the workplace. They both radiate joy and get a kick out of exploring new ideas. They're great at getting things done—as long as they like what they're doing. They're outgoing, curious, and extremely adaptable. Sevens are naturally resilient, so they're well suited for an environment that changes often. Energetic and worldly, they make an experienced and optimistic team.

CHALLENGES

Sevens don't like feeling bored or doing monotonous tasks, so they can lose focus on the task at hand. If they have to work on something for long periods of time, they'll become restless and anxious. They might become acrimonious toward each other in an attempt to vent their frustration. If one suggests an idea or a course of action and the other isn't on board with it, they are likely to be a little selfish and do it the way they please instead. Due to their high energy and insatiable need for variety, two Sevens working together can cause utter chaos in an office.

CONFLICT RESOLUTION

Sevens will need to learn how to take turns sharing their ideas, listening intently, and providing feedback in order to show they are truly being attentive. Neither of them likes too much structure, but they will need to encourage each other to stay focused in order to complete projects. This may require holding each other accountable and checking in with each other to see if there is a way they can help. When their frustration builds, they shouldn't ignore conflict. If they air grievances right then and there, they can quickly address things and move on.

TYPE SEVEN & TYPE EIGHT

STRENGTHS
- Decisive and resilient
- Strong-willed
- Action-oriented and assertive

CHALLENGES
- Defiant and impulsive
- Highly outspoken and blunt
- Push themselves too hard

WORKING IN HARMONY

Sevens and Eights bring an abundance of energy to the workplace. They are both "doers" and do not like to be sitting down all day; they like to be in motion and productive. Sevens enjoy working alongside Eights because of their play-hard attitude, which aligns well with Sevens, who get bored easily. Eights appreciate that Sevens can keep up with them to get things done. Together, they make a high-energy and independent team.

CHALLENGES

Problems arise for these two when they've pushed themselves beyond healthy limits and become stressed and physically exhausted. This can bring out their challenging sides. Sevens become restless and sometimes even manic, which will drive Eights crazy because they're unable to rely on them. At some point, Sevens need to meet face to face with impatient and angry Eights. It may not go well—these two have a tendency to get into very heated arguments.

CONFLICT RESOLUTION

Sevens and Eights should keep track of when they need a break; this will help diminish the likelihood of them getting into arguments. If they do end up in conflict, they'll both need to avoid using coarse language toward each other. Sevens are great at keeping things positive; Eights are skillful at being pragmatic and fair. It's best if they hear each other out and then proceed to find a resolution or compromise.

TYPE SEVEN & TYPE NINE

STRENGTHS
- Highly adaptable
- Friendly and optimistic
- Upbeat and generous

CHALLENGES
- Neglect their responsibilities
- Not great on follow-through
- Conflict-avoidant

WORKING IN HARMONY

Sevens and Nines are a highly compatible match at work. They have complementary attributes that help balance their challenges. They're both sociable and thrive in an environment that is positive and fun. When these two work together on projects, they enjoy bouncing around ideas and getting creative. Sevens like working with Nines because they're easygoing and will go along with other people's ideas or plans to avoid conflict. Nines enjoy having Sevens at work because of their fun and lively spirit. They are an adaptable and creative team.

CHALLENGES

Because these two tend to cultivate a positive attitude and prefer to keep things on the lighter side, they may overlook potential problems that are right in front of them. Nines, if they see conflict, will withdraw and avoid, whereas Sevens tend to just reframe negatives into positives. At work, they have a tendency to miss deadlines and may not follow guidelines due to their avoidant nature.

CONFLICT RESOLUTION

Sevens and Nines are another pair who avoid conflict, so it will be imperative for them to keep communication open. Sevens need to be careful that they are not running over Nines with their high energy. They should make an effort to check in with Nines and encourage them to share their thoughts and ideas. Nines should keep in mind that unless they speak up about a situation that is bothering them, Sevens may not even realize something is wrong. They'll need to stand their ground and be direct to get Sevens' attention.

TYPE EIGHT & TYPE EIGHT

STRENGTHS
- Action-oriented
- Make great leaders
- Committed and honest

CHALLENGES
- Trust and control issues
- Insensitive and blunt
- Combative and reactive

WORKING IN HARMONY

Eights make extraordinary leaders at work. They are strong-minded, determined, and carry themselves with abundant self-confidence. When they work together, amazing things can happen. They're the kind of people who lead movements, alter rules, and make actual change happen, no matter what challenges they face. Together, this team is powerful and indomitable.

CHALLENGES

Serious issues come up for these two when they work together. Under stress, they can become argumentative, challenging, and unkind toward one another. They are both confrontational and will not back down from a provocation. They both want control and seek power to make decisions on their own terms, so if they don't agree on how something should go down, it will likely turn into a battle. Given their extreme and combative nature, when tensions rise, these two are inclined to have some very explosive fights.

CONFLICT RESOLUTION

For Eights at work, it's important that they become aware of how their own high energy levels and intensity can affect those around them. They should also understand the full extent of their strengths and weaknesses. It's essential for Eights to practice self-awareness by restraining the impulses that rise up in their bodies. They are passionate people with strong convictions, so both of them need to communicate with each other in a calm manner. They should always respect the other's need for the same power and control they themselves seek.

TYPE EIGHT & TYPE NINE

STRENGTHS	CHALLENGES
• Persistent	• Lack physical awareness
• Instinctual and loyal	• Stubborn and controlling
• Generous	• False pride

WORKING IN HARMONY

At work, Eights and Nines are both practical, which makes it easier for them to complete tasks and handle projects. They have the ability to balance out the other's challenges: Nines' peaceful and calming presence steadies Eights' high energy; Eights' self-assertive demeanor rubs off on Nines, who can be timid and hesitant to voice their opinions at work. They are a steadfast and supportive team.

CHALLENGES

Eights and Nines can get stuck in a problematic, repeating cycle of dominance and intimidation. Eights can be quite domineering and controlling when it concerns how they think things should be done at work. Nines, feeling intimidated by Eights' aggressiveness, may want to retreat. In turn, Eights will consider this behavioral pattern a sign of weakness from Nines. In order to behave professionally in a work environment, both of them hide their anger, but their resentment will eventually emerge passive-aggressively. Eventually, they become resistant to working alongside each other due to their contrary approaches.

CONFLICT RESOLUTION

In order for Eights and Nines to cooperate at work, they must establish respect and build trust as soon as possible. Eights can begin to build trust with Nines by being encouraging and checking in with Nines to see if they want to share anything. If Nines don't want to share, Eights should avoid pressuring them and, instead, let them know they can come to them at any time. This allows Nines to feel safe. Nines, in turn, build trust with Eights when they firmly stand by their thoughts and opinions. In return, Eights are more apt to respect and trust Nines who stand up for themselves.

TYPE NINE & TYPE NINE

STRENGTHS
- Practical approach to difficult situations
- Approachable and kind
- Accommodating and helpful

CHALLENGES
- Conflict-avoidant
- Difficulty prioritizing
- Stubborn and passive-aggressive

WORKING IN HARMONY

Nines thrive in a quiet and soothing work environment. They prefer to work where there is not a lot of stress or pressure. Right from the start, Nines enjoy a mutual understanding of where the other is coming from. They're both kind and considerate of each other's ideas and naturally get along under most circumstances. They're both positive-minded people who will help each other catch up when they fall behind on work. They are a patient and nonjudgmental team.

CHALLENGES

When they are stressed, Nines become withdrawn and indecisive; when they are absolutely overwhelmed, they shut down. They want to avoid conflict with each other or with an assignment they're working on together so much that they tend to neglect small issues. They struggle with how to prioritize tasks and take initiative. They might even become quietly angry or resentful of the other person. Though Nines aren't inclined to let their anger show, their passive-aggressive behavior will ultimately undercut their productivity.

CONFLICT RESOLUTION

Nines can help motivate each other, especially when they are working under stress. They need to understand the motives behind their inclination to retreat and shut down during tension and conflict. Once they determine why this happens, they can develop a way to stay present, persevere, and follow through on their work. They can help each other do this by sharing their inspiration, support, and positivity. As soon as they feel secure with each other, Nines still need to work on avoiding becoming codependent.

INDEX